For Maggie

WaveMaker: career secrets of outstanding performers

from analysis made in HP and Microsoft

By

Robin Farmer

Contents

Preface

I once heard someone deliver a throwaway one-liner. It was a cliché of course, but it stuck in my head. The line was, "Find your ideal job and you'll never work a day in your life." As I later discovered, this advice is not as idealistic as it first sounds.

Finding a sequence of ideal jobs is what makes a career.

Careers are what we all invest our energy and emotions in, either positively or negatively. Positive being the belief that we can make significant progress in this or another organisation and that it will give us the wherewithal to have a happy and productive life. Negative in that we can feel that everyone is out to get us, and the slippery pole has been freshly greased to scupper us. That it's a "not what you know but who you know" world, and, unfortunately, you don't know anyone. That life's a bitch and then you die!

This book can help both of these beliefs, although, together, we'll spend more time focussing on the former. Focussing on the positive belief that you are in control of your career.

After all, a stellar career is just a sequence of perfect roles.

Many of us will either recall, or even currently be in, a perfect role. Finding this perfect role can be down to luck, happenstance or good fortune. However, isn't it also possible that you engineered the job, or manipulated the universe to make your perfect job happen to you?

Unfortunately, however it came about, many of us see a perfect role as a one-off or, at the very least, a rarity. Finding our perfect job will probably happen to us all at some stage in our careers, but the likelihood of this role lasting or being easily repeatable in today's ever-changing world is most unlikely because, well, stuff changes.

Change is a constant, and change will inevitably impinge on your perfect job. The management will change, the strategy will change, the products will change, and the budget will reduce (it always reduces, trust me on this).

You also know that the likelihood of just stepping from one perfect job straight into another one is slim. After all, if you think about it, your perfect job came about due to complete randomness: a chance meeting, a call from a head-hunter out of the blue, your mate or partner mentioning an opportunity, or the tap on the shoulder by an ex-colleague who moved on two years ago.

Randomness is a conundrum for many of us because it seems to be so … random. Most of the people I have coached over the past 35 years have struggled with this scenario. Far too many of them become convinced there's a conspiracy in the organisation, clandestine meetings with "star chamber" managers in darkened rooms deciding on people's futures and fortunes. If you're not "in" then you're "out". It all seems so random and unfair.

All of this convinces them that their next perfect job is completely out of their control. Repeating the strange alignment of planets, asteroids and magnetic fields that created their last perfect role is beyond their magical powers.

However…

Finding a perfect role turns out to be something that a number of people have discovered how to do repeatedly. Indeed, the number of people who have discovered how to do this, who have discovered the key, is larger than you think. How do I know this? Well, in your head, look upwards into the leadership of your organisation. Almost all of them have found the key or one of the keys.

Understanding what and how these clever folk do it has been a life's work for me, and if you read on, you'll see that it's not as difficult as you thought.

You can achieve your perfect job time and time again by understanding what these clever folk, or stellar performers as I call them, do on a daily basis.

Who is this book for?

Although the statistics tell us that the economy is supported by small businesses, a great many of us work in big corporations and government entities. These organisations are largely populated by people who have decided that the best places to prosper (or perhaps to garner the skills necessary to go it alone in the future) are huge organisations.

Most of these corporations have regimented and structured career paths or role descriptions that map out the career stages and steps available to personnel.

Anyone in such a corporate structure is a prime candidate for this book. Why? Because we will all have noticed one or two individuals who seem to be able to override the strictures and planned career progress stages published on the HR intranet site.

If you spend your working day in a government organisation, you will also have a structured role progression laid out for you, not necessarily dictated by your qualifications and experience (although this is true in the healthcare sector), but heavily influenced by it. However, you will have seen people defy the laws of gravity in these organisations. Those people who seem to be in the right place at the right time, those people who have "connections" that give them an advantage.

These people, whether they be in the corporate world or public sector, have discovered the key to developing a stellar career. They've found the magic formula.

So if you're not content with following the steady planned pattern proposed for all employees, this book is for you. That's because I'll show you exactly what those few folk, who slip upwardly through the company strata in an apparently frictionless manner, are doing differently to the rest of us.

This book is for you because, as you read on, you'll discover that these places of work are also places for careers to develop and grow. You'll discover that building a sequence of ideal roles – what I call the WaveMaker approach – will unlock much more than was first hinted at in your neophyte induction day.

You'll learn the key elements of this approach to career enhancement and get simple but effective tips and exercises that will enable you to take advantage of the formula – quickly, effectively and repeatedly.

What have you got to lose?

Chapter 1. Introducing the formula that will transform your career

Over the past 35 years of managing people, I have picked up a few simple yet valuable concepts that helped me develop my skills as a manager and leader, but mainly as a coach.

You see, what I learned changed my own behaviour toward people, not only in a career sense but also in how I developed my business and client base when the opportunity arose. It certainly enabled me to develop more successfully as a sales manager at Hewlett-Packard. It also helped me make the leap out of HP into running a start-up and ultimately even helped me to sell that start-up. It also created the opportunity to change my technology focus from hardware at HP to software in my start-up and ultimately led to my gaining a position in Microsoft UK.

My motivation to seek out these insights came from trying to better coach the people who reported to me. Although I was a very experienced sales person and was fast gaining experience as a sales manager, I was struggling to coach people on how to do their jobs better. The market was changing and they needed me to be a sales manager. This meant helping them with broader client strategy as opposed to closing their deals. I also needed to lift my focus from individual client activity to the overall business requirements of my team. I had to make a choice: go back to being a successful sales person or learn properly how to succeed through others. For the latter, I needed a better understanding of how to motivate people to deliver their best for me.

Just being above them on the corporate ladder wasn't enough. At best they would pay lip service to my demands, at worst simply ignore me and aim for their sales targets (because, in our company, reaching targets made people bomb-proof). I soon found that by focussing more on their career aspirations, I got their attention. Discussing how best to achieve their career aims changed my relationship with them from deal police to their manager and leader. Don't get me wrong here, the business goal was the same and the discipline of sales management didn't get dropped. What changed was the levers I pulled to get the most out of each individual. I had found that focussing on career coaching and planning gave me a better understanding of the people I managed, and seemed to motivate them positively, leading to increased performance.

The most common career questions I got revolved around advancement and opportunities. "How do I get a promotion?" was one of the questions I was regularly asked. I also often got questions about where the opportunities for learning and advancement came from (as they were not always obvious). My all-time favourite, however, was, "There's obviously a secret society in this place, making decisions about people, right? How can I access it?"

Initially, all I could do was give the pat responses I had been trained to give. I even used the jargon taught to me. "Create a five-year goal-oriented career plan", do more "skip" level meetings to tell your manager's manager about yourself, and the most unhelpful, "develop your elevator pitch" to get your USP over to them. I delve into all this jargon below.

Finding my own coaching formula

Interestingly, I had already worked out that the received wisdom-based activities (five-year plan, elevator pitch to trapped executives, etc.) didn't work for me personally because:

- In the high-growth, high-tech industry I worked in, the concept of a five-year plan was daft. Things moved way too fast. By the way, "goal-oriented" was used in everything from company strategy through to reducing the amount of money spent on photocopying. Goal-oriented was nothing but word stuffing, used to fill out empty statements because it sounds more impressive than "for a good reason".

- Forcing my presence on busy skip-level managers (i.e. those that managed my manager) made me cringe as they always wanted to know the agenda for our meeting. As the agenda was **me, me, me!** I was understandably uneasy.

- And as for my "elevator" pitch (the idea of "selling yourself" to a trapped executive in the lift), it was pretty unappealing to both parties and cringingly awful to others stuck in the lift with you. It just seemed like boasting (not something an English person finds comfortable).

- Similarly awkward was the USP (unique sales proposal), which involves "selling yourself" to emphasise why you are uniquely suited to absolutely everything that the hapless, trapped executive might need.

The combination of being uneasy with the concepts I'd been trained to use, coupled with my own lack of belief in them, led me to lift my head up from my day-to-day role and look for a formula that addressed these challenges. I needed to believe in this formula. I needed something that resonated better with my own experiences.

The answer was right in front of me

To get a better understanding, I went to an experienced manager that had helped me progress and asked for her advice. Interestingly, she suggested I meet with a very senior UK manager that she knew, as that very senior manager had helped her progress. She also asked me where I lived (a long way away on the South Coast). She advised me to try to mention this in our meeting…

The very senior manager I met with was renowned in HP as the next potential President of Office Products (a huge growth area for HP). This was a stellar role in HP Global. He was quite happy to meet me as I had been introduced to him (the reason for this is explained in Chapter 4). I did what I had been told to do, and when he mentioned that he was a keen sailor, I let it be known that I lived on the South Coast and had a small sailing boat myself. I had pushed one of his favourite conversation buttons simply by asking questions about, well, him.

Within minutes of meeting, we were talking about the cost of deep water moorings in the Solent area, where I kept my boat, and her ability to sit on a drying mooring, all because he was a keen sailor. I also got to ask him his opinion on the career training available to new managers ("I wouldn't know, I've never bothered," was his answer). And I asked what his approach to career advancement was.

This is what he told me: "Only do roles that 'float your boat." Again, he couldn't resist the sailor talk. "Work hard to stay relevant to the business and constantly make new connections."

I was in the right place at the right time

It was pure fortune that, while I was pondering these things, I was working in a progressive, flat and open management environment: HP in the 1980s. HP had decided on, and ruthlessly implemented, a flat management structure. This gave me – as a fledgling junior manager and generally nosey person – the ability to identify, observe and even question more stellar management high fliers on their career approach. I met with them using the same strategy that had worked with the recently promoted, sailing enthusiast President of Office Products, and simply asked them about themselves, usually opening with simple questions like "How are you?" or even "What plans do you have for the weekend?" (Turn to Chapter 4 for more on making these meetings work for you.)

What I learned changed my approach to my own career.

I also later learned that what I was doing to research these ideas was changing my brand in a way that I hadn't anticipated. I was gaining a reputation as a successful career coach. This was because what I learned changed the advice and coaching I gave – known as a "feed forward loop" in the tech world.

Over time, this approach got more structured and refined. I was also now able to identify when others were using these techniques around me. I could now observe apparently random interactions and exchanges among the people around me with a new lens – almost X-Ray vision – giving me a clearer insight into what was actually going on. This feedback reinforced my belief in my theory.

"Find the right job and you'll never work a day in your life"

What I observed and learned from talking to the stellar performers in HP, and later on in Microsoft, was that there is a formula based on some very simple techniques that, if applied properly, will accelerate promotion, cause great opportunities to be revealed to you and ensure that your capabilities remain relevant to the business.

Not a bad formula for a fulfilling career.

What is this remarkable formula? It breaks down into just three simple approaches that can deliver the career growth that you're looking for. Just three simple techniques, each of which are explored in depth in this book. They are:

- Fully understand your own core needs and requirements from any role and don't compromise.

- Be completely responsible, clear and consistent with your own brand, and constantly hone it.

- There absolutely is a secret network operating in your organisation – use it!

Together, these three elements make up the WaveMaker approach. You can use any of the above three elements individually but, as we'll see in Chapter 5, consistently combining all three together will "turbocharge" your results.

That's because each aspect of the WaveMaker approach is intertwined with the other two. The effect of the whole is greater than that of the individual parts.

This approach changed my own career and taught me two valuable lessons. First, this approach is insanely effective and powerful, and it can work just as well for you, too. Second, you have to keep doing each component constantly for the effect to keep working.

Why WaveMaker? Because a good career strategy is just like surfing

Like many things in life, careers don't actually exist as an entity. You can't pick them up, you can't smell them and you can't catch them in a jar. Corporations and organisations are merely an illusion created by a collection of likeminded energetic people – if they all changed their minds tomorrow and focussed their energy somewhere else, the corporation would disappear and, like poor old Ozymandias, turn back into sand. What they have in common is energy. Energy created, sustained and propagated by people.

Waves are the same thing. Waves are just energy passing through water, solids or the vacuum of space. Be they huge or small, powerful or weak, destructive or beneficial, they are just energy. Careers are simply a different form of wave energy, passing through the medium of people.

The career strategy of stellar performers, as opposed to almost everyone else, is to maximise that energy in a beneficial way to assist them in their goals. They do this by adopting the strategy of a surfer. This is a strategy that can work for you, as well.

Surfing waves as a career strategy and the "S" curve

HP was a product company and, as such, in my roles as sales person and sales manager, I was constantly bombarded with the product adoption "S" (sigmoid) curve.

The S curve, a mathematical model also known as the logistic curve, describes the growth of one variable in terms of another variable over time. S curves are found in all sorts of fields, from biology and physics to business and technology. In business, the S curve is used to describe, and sometimes predict, the performance of a company or product over a period of time.

The full S curve can be found in the standard deviation "bell curve" that most of us have seen. In HP, we understood the concept for market penetration of a new technology product as shown in Figure 1.

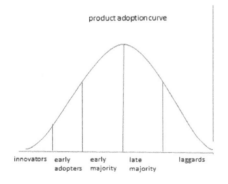

Figure 1. The product adoption S curve

The other S curve that became important to me was the innovation and product development curve, as seen in Figure 2.

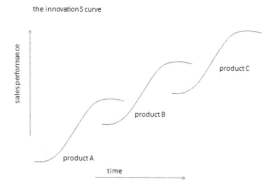

Figure 2. The innovation S curve

This series of curves shows that, to survive in an innovative market, new products have to be created and developed well in advance of the peak of the previous product. If you don't, you run out of market or you run out of cash.

The idea of applying this S curve to careers came from the comments of one of the stellar performers I interviewed in the early stages of my research. When I asked what prompted her to move from career stage to career stage, she described the S curve as a wave and said, "I see myself as a surfer, riding the best waves available and moving to better waves when I find them."

In that way, the S curve is just a wave. Swap "product" for "role" and you have the basis of WaveMaker. The S curve sequence also clearly shows that the best time to start the next role curve is well before the first curve peaks.

Waves as an analogy worked really well for me. And it got me thinking ... if, for a surfer, close to the crest of the wave was the best place to be for maximum energy, it was also the best place to be if you want to move to another, better, wave.

The wave analogy worked brilliantly for stellar performers, but it also worked brilliantly for the not-so-stellar performers. It explained an awful lot about those that couldn't pick the right wave to surf and for those that stayed on a wave past its crest.

You see, what makes the greatest surfer isn't just their surfing skill. It's mostly to do with their ability to choose the best waves to ride. This is what gave me the insight to coach people – not on developing better surfing skills, but to help them develop their wave sense, to make better decisions on which wave to ride. This idea is what changed the way I looked at stellar performers. It's what helped me better understand their behaviour. They weren't just clever and lucky, they were doing something different when it came to identifying the best waves.

With the people I managed, the difference between most of my poorer career performers and my stellar performers seemed to come down to their strategy around waves and opportunities.

Just in front of the crest of a wave, the surfer is looking forward and around to better identify the next wave. At or past the crest of a wave, the surfer is either just looking behind them or trying to survive the inevitable drowning.

Because waves are just energy, this energy can be supplied to a surfer by the wave (surfing) or it can sap the surfer's energy (swimming against the current). At the right point on the wave, the wave gives the surfer the energy they need to move forward. However, if they hang on for too long, the surfer ends up supplying energy to the wave, trying to keep it going. They get drained of energy and can't succeed. Hanging on to a dwindling wave for too long is one of the major reasons for a failing career strategy.

Leaving the stellar performers to their fun for a second, let's explore the struggling performer.

Comparing successful surfers with struggling surfers

It was so obvious to me when I compared and contrasted the two "surfer" types: successful and struggling.

The struggling performer/surfer is so spent of energy, having invested it in a failing wave, that they become negative and start to think like a victim – "I've given this wave my all. I've been loyal and committed to making it a success. Now no one cares." In fact, they seek out others who sound and behave like they do. Unfortunately, this is where they get most of their advice from, which only makes things worse. Their Hubs (see Chapter 4) are likeminded folk, and they have little energy or interest in expanding their network outside of their own beliefs. The wave they are on is fast becoming irrelevant to the organisation, so they spend lots of energy telling the organisation that it is wrong! The organisation's response to this creates an overpowering sense of injustice in them, driving their behaviour further below the surface. They go on a crusade doing all the wrong things for the "right" reasons.

For them, at this point, in the trough of the passing wave, they start making even worse decisions (if that's at all possible). At this point **any other wave** is better than the one they're on. They are disconnected from the right Hubs, being advised by other negative people and dismissive of good advice. They try to move away from this place. Every role move they make goes hideously wrong for them, damaging themselves and their brand. The only strategy they have is an "away from" their current predicament. They have no real goal and no vision of themselves.

In contrast to this, the stellar performers are whooping and shouting about how great life is. They attract attention because of their positivity and energy. They're riding a brilliant wave and everyone with ambition wants to be with them. People are drawn to the wave they are on and are clamouring to join them and then ... they jump to another role that no one saw coming (or may even seem like a backward step). They have left a brilliant wave just before its crest. They have joined another wave that, over time, screams past the previous wave, lifting them higher in the organisation. They do this time and time again.

How do the stellar performers achieve this?

Quite simply, they used the three steps I mentioned earlier, the WaveMaker formula for career growth:

- Fully understand your own core needs and requirements from any role and don't compromise.

- Be completely responsible, clear and consistent with your own brand, constantly honing it.

- There absolutely is a secret network operating in your organisation – use it!

Let's take a brief look at each of the three steps these stellar career performers were routinely performing.

Understand your core needs

It's important to fully understand the needs that a role must deliver for you (note I said it must deliver *for you*, not the other way around). We often look at a career opportunity from the perspective of "can I do this job?" but we seldom ask ourselves "will it meet my needs?" If these needs are being properly met, then your performance will be at its peak. I found the stellar performers focussed not on "do I have the capability to deliver what this role requires?" but instead "will this role meet my requirements?" I initially found this position perplexing and quickly concluded that, to get on in management, you needed to be breathtakingly arrogant! But it isn't that simple. Understanding your own needs from a role perspective turns out to be the most telling driver for your career decision making. Not having this understanding leads to some classic career-killing situations. Turn to Chapter 2 for more on understanding your needs.

Hone your personal brand

Personal brand is now a hackneyed and over-used phrase. This is mainly because it was pitched as a standalone quick fix to all career issues; plus, it was easy to deliver in a half-day training course, so became the poster child for HR development plans. However, my observation of the stellar performers was that they didn't keep mentioning their brand but seemed to have a clear and consistent way to present and project it all the time.

The other thing that was clear was that they made a direct connection between reputation and brand, protecting their reputation as part of their overall brand. The interesting thing about this whole reputation and brand thing was the behaviour of so-called "high fliers". These folk clearly utilised some of the behaviours of the stellar performers, but always moved role before the damage they caused caught up with them. This was generally an open secret to the masses, but apparently not to senior managers. However, karma will get you in the end and ultimately the high flier's reputation within the organisation got destroyed by this strategy – although they had usually moved organisation by this point. Unfortunately, for those left behind, the high flier's visibility and ultimate demise caused the masses to adopt them as their poster child for "why not to be ambitious". Turn to Chapter 3 for more on developing your reputation and brand.

Use the secret network in your own organisation

There is a secret network operating in your organisation. In fact, there are numerous secret societies working 24x7. They are constantly influencing the decisions made that impact you, and can work against you or for you. That is a definite, is provable and can be easily tested.

Now, you can throw your hands in the air, scream "I BLOODY KNEW IT!!" and blame all your misfortune on this. Or, like ALL secret societies, you can learn the secret handshake. Turn to Chapter 4 to see how.

Finally, and I cannot stress this enough, these three steps are interlinked. Stellar performers use all three together all of the time, and they don't cherry pick the bits they fancy. So don't try one aspect in isolation, and don't use this approach once and turn it off after you see results. Keep using WaveMaker, and you'll be able to keep the momentum going and achieve maximum results. Find out how to use all these strategies together and keep the momentum going in Chapters 5 and 6.

Now, how do you take these ideas on board and use them to change your own career trajectory? Read on and it all becomes clear.

Notes.

Chapter 2. Understanding your own core needs and requirements

One of the main tenets of Neuro-Linguistic Programming (NLP) is the concept of identifying something successful that someone does really well and copying it (apologies to my NLP friends for that insultingly simple summary!). This part of the WaveMaker formula is based on that simple premise, and some of the techniques explained in this chapter are based on NLP.

Most of us don't put too much effort into properly understanding our feelings or finding words to describe our needs (especially, dare I say it, British males). However, the stellar career performer seems to instinctually understand what their ideal role should offer them for their success. They understand their core needs from any role.

Because many of us don't have this instinct – or more likely have had it "parented out of them" (see the poem *This be the Verse* by Philip Larkin) – I needed to find a way to coach people back into this way of thinking.

Here's how I do it.

Understanding your needs

We all have a time in our working life when everything went right. You know, we were working on a critical project, or in a great team or in a brilliant role, and our objective was simple: to change the world in a big or small way. Those were the times when there weren't enough hours in the day, when we couldn't wait to get back to work in the morning. Time rushed by, the energy levels were high and nothing got in the way … not even the "management".

Remember that time, that project, that team, that goal?

Take yourself back to that time, that perfect time. Soak it up. Remember the sounds, the smells, even the tastes (cake and champagne?). That was a perfect project, the perfect role for you.

A light comes on somewhere inside you.

Imagine that there are a number of red LED lights inside your head. Like the lights on your car dashboard. Each one of these LEDs is wired to a complex, almost infinitely convoluted circuit within your brain. And each LED has a label under it denoting what it means to you when it lights up, when the circuit is stimulated. If you have an LED that lights up because your team leader congratulates you for doing an excellent job, the likelihood is that the "label" under that LED says "valued". Feeling valued is therefore one of your core needs. If you get a great feeling from seeing your name on the list of distinguished engineers for your company, then it's likely that one of your LED labels says "respected".

Now, remember the feelings that the above perfect role stirred in you? Chances are, at least five or six of those LEDs are burning brightly. Why do I say that? My coaching experience shows that, to feel the way you did back then, you need at least that number of LEDs to be lit up. In other words, you need five or six of your core needs to be properly met for you to feel happy and fulfilled in a role.

It's not difficult to also see that, when just one of these brightly burning LEDs starts to flicker or blink out completely, it is immediately noticeable. This loss of one or more LEDs can be triggered when your role changes, or the organisation around you changes or you are nearing the end of a project. You know you feel uneasy, but you're not entirely sure why; you know you feel vulnerable or unsure of the future, but can't identify exactly why...

You feel that way because your LEDs have started blinking out. But which ones?

To understand which LEDs are causing you concern, you need to fill in the label under as many LEDs as you can. That's something we can do together.

<u>How to understand and name your LEDs</u>

To identify your personal LED labels, you need to understand how you felt during your perfect project or role, as this can reveal a great deal about what makes you happy. This requires a little imaginative regression, so bear with me for a few minutes.

Think back to that perfect role. Where were you and what were you doing? Think about the role or project for a few minutes and answer the following questions:

- What were you responsible for?
- Were you on your own or in a team? If you were part of a team, what role did you play?
- Was the objective clear to you and did it make you feel good?

Now, let's start picking things apart in more detail. I'll assume that, if you were in an organisation, you were part of a successful team. So, based on that:

- Was your opinion and contribution wanted and listened to?
- Did you get the chance to shape the outcome?
- Did the goal/end result resonate with you?
- Were you making a difference to people?
- Were your ideas followed by others?
- Were you responsible for a significant part of the outcome?
- Were you leading others?
- What did the team think of you, and what did you think of them?
- Were you supported by your managers?

Let's pick that list apart for a little more insight.

Your opinion and contribution were wanted, yes? Okay then, what did you get from that? It felt good, yes? But what else? Did it make you feel important? No? Okay then, what did YOU get from it? You felt valued. Great, let's save VALUED as a label and move on.

Did you get the chance to shape the outcome? Assuming you did, what did shaping the outcome get for you? Yes, it felt good, but what else? You felt able to change the direction when needed. Okay good, what did that get for you? The leadership looked to you for advice? Great, but what did YOU get from it? You felt respected. And that was what made you feel good? Okay, let's save RESPECT and move on.

Did the goal/end result resonate with you? (Well of course it did, otherwise you wouldn't have picked this scenario, but I'll ask anyway.) What did this resonating goal get for you? Let's make the assumption that it felt good, as that's a given when an LED comes on. But what did it get for YOU? Clarity. Excellent. What did having a clear, resonating goal get for you? You could see what you were moving toward, and it was positive. And what did that get for you? Vision. Okay, let's save VISION and move on.

All a bit repetitive, eh? In the coaching process, repetitiveness is essential. Besides, although the questions are the same, the "journey" that a coachee takes is different each time because the starting point is different. Even if some of the LED labels are the same, the route to get there will be different for each person.

Looking at labels and their sources

Below is a list of the labels and their associated sources that my coachees have found. It's not exhaustive but it should give you a good feel for identifying and understanding your own labels. In my coaching career, I have seen many, many different interpretations of the labels identified. But this is a book, not an individual two-hour coaching session, so I've boiled it down in a way that works for most people. If you find your own different labels, that's absolutely fine and dandy.

- Leading the team or project – defining the direction – being in control – CONTROL.
- Being left alone by management to do the job – getting all the resources needed – being empowered – POWER.
- Your opinion and expertise is asked for – you are listened to – you get respect – RESPECT.
- The project goal was good and positive – you were making the world better – pride in your objective – positive common goal – you knew what you were there to do and it had meaning – PURPOSE.
- Responsible for developing the graduates – loved helping people learn – teaching was rewarding – I walked eight miles through thick snow because my patients need me – VOCATION.
- It was a great team – you belonged – part of a family – worked hard, played hard – felt … VALUED.
- No one has ever done this before – leading-edge technology – big learning curve – PERSONAL GROWTH.
- Taking on very risky challenges – exciting and visible – in a competitive environment – if we pull this off we'll be heroes and can write our own ticket – down to me to make this happen – staying ahead of your own competition – SECURITY.
- Healthcare/defence/customer-focussed – for the good of the country – highly confidential – saving lives – DUTY.

This is not an exhaustive list, and in my coaching work I often find subtle differences due to the thinking of the coachee. But hopefully you can get my drift. Now, let's look at why the most common labels matter so much to us.

POWER. This doesn't mean you're a power-hungry nutter. More, without access to resources and funds, your vision can't be achieved.

GROWTH. Moving forward and keeping ahead of the technology/subject. An achievement in itself.

CONTROL. Not being a control freak but keeping a steady hand on the tiller, navigating safely to the waypoint, keeping the sails full of wind, a flappy sail is an unhappy sail, etc. (Sailor-speak is obviously contagious.)

VALUED. Everyone likes to feel wanted and needed, part of the solution.

VISION. Speaks for itself, but the vision doesn't have to be a high, snow-capped peak. It may be a tiny flower growing in the dark. Not all visions need to be lofty or "big picture". I have worked with many program managers who see a bug-free code build at the close of day as nirvana.

PURPOSE. We all need a purpose in life. Why shouldn't this apply to our working life as well?

VOCATION. Teachers, doctors, nurses and anyone who gets a kick from helping others for little return is driven by vocation.

DUTY. You don't need to "die in a ditch", but a sense of duty is a powerful motivation, whether it be to our country, to our customers or to our mates.

SECURITY. For most of us working in a highly competitive environment (or should I say all of us) seeking out bleeding-edge technology, risky projects or highly visible/brave endeavours – and succeeding – makes us more secure in our career.

RESPECT. As Joni Mitchell sang in *Big Yellow Taxi*, "You don't know what you got 'til it's gone." Respect is akin to this. When you have it, you don't necessarily pay much attention to it, but you sure know how you feel if you lose it.

TRUST. Trust in the goals of the project and the behaviour of those around you. Trust in your employer.

TRUSTED. Everyone loves being micro-managed, right? Especially by someone new to the company who has no idea of what's going on!! (Ooops, did I say that out loud?) It's quite easy to identify when this particular LED blinks out. The challenge is what to do about it without behaving like a four-year-old!

Your task, before we move on, is to try to go through the process above to:

- Identify your perfect project or role in the past.
- Tease out what you were actually doing and why.
- Link these activities to your inner core needs by repeating the "what did it get for you?" question until you arrive at the labels on your LEDs. Aim to identify five or six of your core needs/LED labels.

Now you know what you need to be successful

What you have now identified, probably for the first time in your life, are the key components that any role HAS to offer you for you to be successful in it. This is the instinctive knowledge that the stellar career performer has at the front of their mind.

You will have experienced the unsettling feeling in the past when something changes in your role or work environment. It makes you feel uneasy. You may not have known why. From now on, you'll be able to step back and analyse your internal LEDs and figure out exactly which one or ones have blinked out.

For example, we've all experienced a sudden change in management. Why should that worry you if your team and project are performing well? *Because the new leadership might want a change in direction?* Maybe your sense of CONTROL LED is blinking? *Perhaps the change means your management sponsor has moved*, which means your POWER LED may be blinking?

Or if a new senior team member joins and doesn't seem to want your advice, maybe your RESPECT LED is blinking. And so on and so on.

Once you can understand what is troubling you, you can take action to correct it, whether that means arranging a meeting with the new manager to brief her on the project, asking if it is still on-mission, asking if the budgets and resources are still available, etc.

When you have let this new self-understanding sink in, you can even use it in a tactical way. At your next meeting (you will always have one coming up), put your LED labels in a list in your notebook (or tablet) and, as the meeting progresses, put a tick on each one that blinks. You'll be surprised at how it helps moderate your response (and you'll surprise your colleagues when you don't storm out halfway through as usual).

Your core needs – how and when to bring them out

When you next have a job interview to attend, or an "informational" meeting with the offering manager, forget all your usual questions about the package or the company. Instead, make a list of questions that relate to your LED labels. Understanding whether the role is right for you to succeed is more important. This behaviour has a double benefit that you might not expect.

It goes like this ... any manager worth their salary will be looking for successful people. This is because any manager worth their salary knows that successful people make them more successful. If you ask a bunch of targeted questions focussed on your own needs for success, the interviewer will notice and they'll want you even more (and package won't get in their way). Why? It's simple human nature really. The person hiring has some core needs, just like you. They will have spent quite a lot of time thinking about, justifying (even if they are replacing a recent leaver) and working with HR to define the role, which means they should be quite clear in their own mind not only what the role needs to deliver, but also how it needs to be done. It's highly likely (unless they are mass-recruiting for expansion) that they have at least one candidate in mind for the role (the reason for this will become clear later in this book).

Your task whenever you interact with the hiring manager is primarily to ensure that all of your LED labels are properly catered for in the role. Proving to the manager (and probably his hiring assessment team) that you have the experience, motivation and ability to deliver the role is obviously critical but it's only part of the issue. If the hiring manager wants you, then a shortfall in your technical knowledge or hands-on project management experience or your direct people leadership experience will be seen as a manageable risk and not a barrier. That's because the hiring manager sees you as a confident, successful person with an excellent understanding of how to be more successful. Why is this?

It's down to the questions you were asking in contrast to the other interviewees.

Asking the right questions

In my roles as sales manager and professional development manager, covering more than 20 years of recruiting, I have interviewed hundreds of people. These people only made it to the interview stage if their CV indicated that they could fit in the organisation's culture and had relevant experience. Interestingly, 90% of CVs fail at this point. Assuming you make it through the CV round, you'll probably be up against internal candidates who have already passed the culture test, but may still need to pass the relevant experience test. I also know that the majority of your competitors will all have been focussed on proving they were capable of doing the job as described. That's assuming they have properly read the job description (again, been there, seen that). They will have come to the interviews in the assessment process either unprepared or totally focussed on the "job at hand". Any questions about what they wanted to achieve in their career, what the next role might be to achieve this and how they have managed their personal development to get there will usually be pretty vague.

Then there is the killer "make or break" question at the end of all of these interviews. It's a question that seems innocuous and friendly but is, in fact, a bear trap hidden under some thin branches. Here's how to spot it … it sounds like this … are you ready? You don't want to miss it. "Thanks for your time and, before we finish, do you have any questions you'd like to ask?" There! Did you see it? Did you see it coming?

"Do you have any questions you'd like to ask?" Holy shit!

Have you prepared or is the only question you have, "Is there a bus to the train station?"

One of the best replies to this I have ever been given was, "Yes I have a question. What would you like me to cover again or explain more fully for me to win this job?" Cooolio! Great question! Put me, the interviewer, on the spot! I didn't hire her for that job but two months later I hired her for a more senior role.

The last question of the day isn't just courtesy. It's an opening, not necessarily a closing. It's the time to ask the question associated with your LEDs. For example, you could ask, "Assuming I'm successful in the role, what are the opportunities for further progression?" which comes from your personal growth LED. Or, "Who would I be reporting to on a daily basis?" which speaks to your power LED. Or "Would I have a say in who works on my projects?" which comes from your control LED.

<u>What your questions say about you</u>

In my experience, self-knowledge and success-oriented questions like these are rare and telling. When I drew my assessment team together at the end of a busy recruitment day, it was questions like these that resonated with all of the assessors. It reeks of success.

Something worth remembering about modern corporate organisations is that their managers are typically very experienced at recruiting. In modern organisations, much of a manager's time is invested in this critical activity, either recruiting externally or internally. They have to be great at it.

If a great manager is recruiting, then he or she is seeking to hire successful people, not just lucky ones.

Most managers worth their salary are testing for and seeking out successful behaviours. Being absolutely clear just why you are successful and making sure you explore your own needs at interview is essential for you. In my experience, the few times this clarity and focus actually comes across in a recruitment assessment process, it tends to infect the interviewers positively. Think about it, working in a global tech company meant that, provided the candidate had the basics and the intellect, even if they weren't up to speed on the latest stuff, there was little risk. After all, I could have them trained easily. However, if I recruited someone with little self-awareness, no self-confidence and a poor understanding of how to survive a corporate environment, then my risk was huge! You have to get across to the recruiting manager that **you understand why you are successful**. Not only does this set you apart from the others, it reduces the risk to the manager when she hires you.

Also remember that, if you are recruited by a successful manager, then they will be a successful Hub in the organisation (see Chapter 4) and are likely to have a very good understanding of career strategy, which should get you off on the right foot.

The danger of compromising

Never compromise on your core needs. If key elements are not in the role, even if the opportunity looks exciting, don't be fooled into taking the role in the hope that those missing things will get fixed downstream. Those missing LEDs will not be lit post joining. It's not a priority to the organisation. Taking a "cool" role, because of the allure of something shiny, and ignoring your core needs is not as uncommon as you'd think. In a fast-moving, innovative organisation, it's easy to be blinded by the new and shiny.

This is a mistake. In fact, the only thing that can destroy a career quicker than hanging on to a hopeless role for too long is chasing after something shiny.

This is most horribly true in the high-tech world that I come from. Why? Because it's full of the shiniest things imaginable. Think of it like this, if you are staring excitedly at something shiny, you are not looking at the person dangling it in front of you! Their agenda is much more important than the shiny thing. If you don't spend time getting to understand their business agenda and the hiring manager's needs, you will not take up a role that meets your needs. It may well be that you could negotiate on the way into such a role to make sure your core needs are met, but you have to be clear on what gaps need addressing. This way, the shiny new thing could be a real lift to your career, not a potential killer.

And if you're already in a role when your LEDs are blinking out, and you can't find a way to get them back on, STOP! You may not be able to fix this. If you try to, you could expound tons of energy trying to get back to where you were. Instead, be proactive, and start looking for your next wave with some urgency.

How *not* to understand your needs and requirements

The world of NLP teaches us that identifying something that works and copying it has great benefit. I have found this to be true, but I have also learned a great deal from understanding the behaviour of those that were failing to achieve their career goals.

In fact, I have observed there is a correlation between career-positive behaviours (like WaveMaker) and career-damaging behaviours. They are direct and inverse. Let me explain...

As you know, I use the analogy of surfing waves as a great explanation of how careers progress, how identifying the next wave and hopping over to it at the right time gives the surfer a constant supply of energy. As these folk power on into their next role (wave) they seem tireless, energised and positive.

However, I have also observed those folk that hang on to the wave they are on for dear life, pouring their own energy into it to try to maintain momentum. They believe that this is the one and only wave for them. It feels safe to them. They fully understand what's needed to be great in this role so they invest their energy and brand in it and show total loyalty to it (either the technology or ethos or market). What they don't seem able to do is take a step back and observe the wave they are riding objectively. It is an easy mistake to make (I know 'cause I've done it myself).

Had they been working with a good mentor, they would have seen the shore and rocks much sooner. But they don't see it. Instead, these folk beach themselves on the sun-baked sand, drying up in the sun, wasting away, with the sound of waves and happy surfers in their sand-filled ears and ... blame everyone else for their decisions.

Observing this is painful but enlightening. The behaviour that these folk exhibit, had they chosen the right wave, would be very successful. They work hard and late into the evening. They can't sleep from trying to fix the issues. They are passionate and energised about their wave. But they start to think like victims.

Victims have a certain type of magnetism. It's incredibly strong but very specific – namely, it's great for attracting other victims. Victims are like Anti-Hubs (see Chapter 4), they connect with each other and start packaging up their paranoia and passing it around. They become seditious, subversive and negative.

It is almost impossible to hide this behaviour. In fact, many become proud of it and actively make it part of their brand!

Worse still, their capabilities and skills are seen as temporarily valuable to the organisation so it tolerates them. This toleration can last years as products and technologies create their own long tail. However, these folk now only have a job, not a career, and their real value to the leading edge of the organisation's focus diminishes.

Coaching folk who have ridden their wave for too long can be frustrating (that's assuming they are aware enough to want to be coached). It takes time for them to let go of their grotty, smelly and decaying comfort blanket. It takes time for them to admit that they don't like where they are.

When they recognise that they are in a bad position, they often pursue the same solution. They apply for any role that comes up, whether suitable or not. They often choose these role opportunities based on their belief that they could do the job, not whether the job suits them. The reason for this behaviour is very simple to understand.

If you believe you are in a bad position, then getting away from it is more pressing than choosing the right place to go. It's called an "away-from" strategy and is far more common than you'd think. In some instances, an away-from strategy is understandable. I found this out when I was diagnosed with cancer. However, it's critical that we recognise this strategy for what it is: uncontrolled flight cause by fright. By the way, this is exactly the time to seek a coach or mentor (or, in my case, a second opinion!).

All of this leads the Non-WaveMaker into the following behaviours:

- They seek out other victims, their own version of Hubs (Anti-Hubs). This reinforces their sense of victimhood.
- They isolate themselves from the leadership team because they distrust them.
- Their body language and verbal language changes, often becoming critical and closed.
- Advice from any remaining mentors is ignored or avoided as it contradicts their world view.
- They work longer and harder to try to keep their wave moving.
- If they manage to move roles, they invariably pick the wrong wave.
- Their energy is sapped. Their brand is damaged.
- Most of their LEDs blink out.

How stellar career performers understand their own needs and requirements

Once I had started to understand what stellar performers were doing, I was able to identify more easily when I witnessed it. When interviewing them and listening to them talk, it was clearer to me how deeply engrained this thinking was for them. Examples of this came thick and fast once I knew what to look for.

For example, I asked a regional sales manager why he had moved to an equivalent level role in marketing (a sideways move), rather than the more linear route through regional and country sales manager. "Sales is really only part of the marketing process," he said. "If we all better understood the whole process then we could take leadership roles anywhere in HP."

I asked, "So does marketing float your boat?" (Once a sailor, always a sailor.)

"Not especially, no," he replied. "But leading a larger, more autonomous part of the business does."

Hmmm, that really got my cogs turning. A sideways move into a related area brought a greater understanding of the business and opened up a window into a broader leadership opportunity. Leadership, power, control, personal growth … all those LEDs are there.

In Microsoft, my group manager made an apparent backward step from Large Enterprise sales management into our Small Business group, to a role I didn't recognise. When I caught up with him and quizzed him on it he said, "There's a big growth opportunity here and the structure is still being defined. It was a great opportunity to help shape the group at a worldwide level, as we are the first region to do this."

Hmmm again. An apparent backward move into a smaller "start-up" group. But lots of growth, first region to try this out, worldwide influence … not opportunities that present themselves often, yet perfectly aligned with his LEDs. And what else? More control, personal growth, meaningful goal/vision, influence and power at a worldwide level. Kind of makes your mouth water, doesn't it?

How do stellar career performers discover opportunities like this? We'll look at that later.

Notes

Chapter 3. Being responsible, clear and consistent with your own brand

Personal brand. We all get it, right?

If only that were true.

The personal brand secret

My observations and interviews with stellar performers revealed something quite exciting about the way they reviewed, honed and communicated their brand. The clue was always in front of me, because I watch TV. After a house, your child's education and possibly divorce, what's the most expensive thing you buy and take the most care buying (perhaps even more care than your house)?

Cars, kitchens and bathrooms.

Focussing on cars, car companies spend a lot of money on advertising. They advertise in all possible mediums, including TV.

Watch a couple of car ads with a different point of view. Forget the fabulous, shiny, desirable, luxury car and look at the advertisement. Notice how they present their product. Notice how they present their brand. They try to present why their brand is *relevant* – be it high-end German engineering and luxury "that straightens bends and shortens straights", or the latest energy-efficient technology that improves the planet, or the safest affordable car you can buy, or the only SUV that can be seen from outer space.

These organisations make sure their brand message is *relevant* to the market they are aiming at. You'd think we all bought cars for different reasons, but it turns out we don't. However, the reasons change over time. As such, car manufacturers constantly spend a fortune trying to better understand our current reasons for buying a car. There's a whole industry focussed on just this. Because, when car companies understand our reasons, they can make sure their brand is relevant to those reasons.

What I discovered in my research is that stellar performers invest in this process of brand relevance in a similarly intensive way. They are constantly refining, checking and researching what the organisation (their market) is doing, thinking and implementing. To keep their brand relevant, they make time (investment) and make efforts to gather and interpret this information. They use it to refine and refocus their own brand as a continuous exercise. Many that I talked to were unaware that they did this explicitly, but their knowledge and deep understanding of their environment was very evident when I asked them about it.

Another revelation that came out of observing stellar performers was the duration of their brand thinking and reviewing. Almost none of them had a five-year plan, because where you want to be in five years is a nonsense in the high-tech and/or fast-moving environments of the 21st century.

This way of thinking about your brand is, for most of us, not a natural state of being. But it can be cultivated with the exercises in this chapter.

Coaching for your "future brand"

First, we'll delve into a few concepts that will be used in the upcoming exercises...

Limiting beliefs

Let's look at some background. You (and I) have things called "limiting beliefs". These limiting beliefs are the rocks strewn all over the road ahead. You have been busily placing them there most of your life. You are good at it and would probably list it among your superpowers. Limiting beliefs are the old wives' tales, received wisdom, common sense and feedstock of the naysayers. They come through clearly as the little voice in the back of your head telling you that you've failed at this before, you haven't got the ability, you will make a fool of yourself and lose all your money. The voice may be your mum's or dad's, it may be a feared teacher, or it may be a critical partner. It may even be you. You can't shut it up, ever.

You're not mad. You are normal.

We need to understand this and be clear on our limiting beliefs for the exercises to work.

Managing a brand

We also need to better understand a role that you have probably never experienced before. This role is a "brand manager". There is something special about a brand manager. They have to fully understand the attributes of the products under the brand (for instance, BMW 1,2,3,4,5,6,7,8 Series all require a different strategy but carry the brand attributes) and be able to focus on the relevant attributes of the individual products.

Some of the most important skills of a brand manager are their clinical, unemotional and ruthless understanding of all aspects of their product – warts and all. Without this detachment they cannot effectively address issues that the market (or their competition) might bring up against them. Think about the new Skoda brand positioning and how the brand managers dealt with the negative connotations of the previous generation of Skoda, i.e. an Eastern bloc joke machine.

My point is, the brand manager must be brutally realistic about how her product is viewed in any market so that they can address the market perception effectively. There would be no point spending resources trying to sell Skodas to BMW 7 Series buyers.

But back to you. Can you be your own brand manager? Can you be unemotionally detached about how you are perceived? Probably not, you think, or not without recreational pharmaceuticals anyway. But the upcoming exercises will help you be your own detached, ruthless brand manager.

Future brand vs reputation

We all have a reputation. All brands have a reputation. Reputation is part of every brand (go back to Skoda and BMW). Reputation is extremely important. When I coach engineers (and software developers, architects, project managers, etc.), they find it hard to detach reputation from their brand's future potential. This is very understandable as often their value as an engineer is predicated on their reputation. However, reputation cannot be used to influence the direction a brand moves in. Only your brand aspiration or "future brand" can do that.

Future brand is conceptual and influences the shape of what the brand delivers in the future. You can see this in the concept vehicles produced by car makers for major trade shows like Geneva, Detroit or London. These are concept cars that incorporate the upcoming technologies and ideas. Many of these become mainstream over time (think Audi TT or Range Rover Evoque), and car companies spend a great deal of their resource on this activity because it pays huge dividends for the brand and for future products.

All of these aspirational brands have something in common – they are all possible. They must be presented in the realm of possibility or the market (and especially the press) will lambast them and damage the car company's reputation and larger brand.

As you'll read later, understanding reputation and brand is important. Remember that your reputation is an intrinsic part of your brand, and reputation can support your future brand or it can undermine it if your reputation doesn't align with your brand aspiration.

I have coached many engineers and architects with exceptionally good reputations in my career, and helping them understand the difference between reputation and brand has been key. You see, if you put energy and time into promoting just your reputation, then you are feeding the network with what you have done in the past. This is excellent (providing it's positive). However, you may be frustrated that this behaviour keeps bringing you opportunities to do more of what you have already proved yourself in.

The stellar performer and their brand

When thinking about the stellar performers I observed and spoke with, there was a definite "positive intervention" approach to their reputation. They would take steps to protect their reputation (what they had achieved) by being particular about who and what they associated with. Their brand, however, was always presented as what they could achieve, not what they had already achieved. Most of all, the stellar performers right across the board wanted to be in control of how they were perceived.

On a few occasions, I saw this behaviour in action in project review meetings. On more than one occasion, a known stellar performer would scan the room early in the meeting, recognise if the attendees and the agenda were going to be agreeable to them and, if not, make an excuse and leave. The advent of the mobile phone had given them a simple and ubiquitous device to extricate themselves from the "wrong" meeting. Nowadays, you don't even need to explain anything other than pretend your phone is active, wave it at the folk in the room, mime "sorry, customer" and just push off.

One particular stellar performer even had a formula for ensuring he was perceived in the right way. One "atta boy" was worth three "oh shits". As you can probably tell, he is American.

I, on the other hand, had an analogue for "deep staff" meetings: pigs and hens. It is based on the "full English" breakfast of eggs and bacon. You see, the hen was involved, but the pig was really committed! Avoid becoming associated with meetings full of hens – they just cluck loudly, crap everywhere and clog things up with feathers.

There is a very simple reason why you should present your future brand (i.e. being clear on what you could achieve). That is, you want to find opportunities to develop and grow new capabilities. You want jobs that fit your aspirations, not roles that you have already proven yourself in. As we'll see in Chapter 4, promoting your future brand is the device that stirs the network into bringing you opportunities for you to grow and develop into.

Exercises: Learning to become your own brand manager

It would be useful, when you do these exercises, to have a large piece of paper or a whiteboard handy. It will help you keep track, and capture the ideas and revelations as they come. You will also need a marker pen, crayon or any old pen.

Now, imagine you are standing on a line on the floor that represents your life, from the start to the ultimate finish (don't dwell on the finish part).

Exercise 1. Bringing out your inner brand manager

Move along on this imaginary line to the point that represents now, today, this instant. Relax there for a second. You now need to observe yourself from another perspective, that of the brand manager. We talked about this perspective earlier. Think of it as a role you are playing (think back to your drama lessons in school). Give your brand manager a different name if it helps. Then imagine, as the brand manager, you can step out of yourself and look back at yourself as a separate person.

Go on try it, look back at yourself. Can you see the emotional baggage piled up all around? As brand manager, you don't have this baggage. As brand manager, you are acutely aware that this baggage is the source of all those limiting beliefs. All those "yes but" concerns that stop progress.

"Yes but," I hear you say. Trust me, run with me on this. I've used this exercise in coaching sessions hundreds of times, and it really works.

As brand manager, you have access to all of the performance data that pertains to the other you in the room. Now is the time to bring it out and analyse it. This data represents the current perspective of your brand in the part of the organisation or company that it lives in (this is your market). Many companies spend millions and millions of dollars surveying their clients to get data like this ... your brand manager gives it to you for nothing!

As the brand manager, start writing on the whiteboard (on the left side, as you'll be needing room later) all of the attributes, positive and negative, that describe the brand as you see it currently. Remember, no one else will see this so be as honest as possible. When I am coaching someone through this exercise, they usually start with the things they have been told that irk them beyond tolerance, followed by things that directly contradict this. This is normal. Stay calm and keep going.

So, for example, a typical coaching session on present brand might shake out as:

- **Negative things about present brand based on feedback:** Long time in role, seen as in a rut, no structure to development plans, limited new feedback, poor interaction with leadership, little evidence of mentoring others.
- **Positive things about present brand based on feedback:** Seen as "expert" in desktop security, presenting in product training, consistent customer satisfaction feedback, very high utilisation levels, puts customer needs first.

This is quite typical of a field- (client-) based technician who is dedicated to client success but with little time or tolerance for schmoozing the bosses.

There will always be positive things and negative things. Remember that managers use "manager speak", so make sure that what was made to sound positive isn't actually negative. You want to avoid things like, "Robin has been in this role for 10 years and is clearly very comfortable with it!"

When you've exhausted your supply of data, step back and look at what you've captured. Should (heaven forbid) someone who knows you come across this list, would they know it was you? If not, try harder.

What you have just done is capture your current brand perception in your immediate market.

Now, go and have a coffee or a tea. Chill and ponder.

Exercise 2. Understanding your aspirational brand

Three, two, one ... you're back in the room. Staying in the role of brand manager, we now embark on the really exciting part of the process: making the brand manager work hard for their exorbitant salary.

Assuming you are standing on the imaginary line that you made for the first exercise, now, as the brand manager, move along it a distance that represents two years into the future. This is now the domain of the near future. As brand manager, it is your job to define where you expect your brand to be at this time and how you expect it to be perceived in the market – assuming you've done your job properly, of course (heaven knows you're paid enough!).

This is about how you want the market to describe your brand, or what your brand represents at this point in the future. Think about what your brand has achieved at this future point. Start writing this on the right-hand side of the whiteboard (or large piece of paper).

My experience when coaching this exercise is that we always start by being very conservative (with a small c), but as the energy aligns with the process, things start to flow. As brand manager, it's also your job to stop the limiting beliefs from getting in the way of progress. As the aspirations come forward, the "yes but" voice will start to inhibit progress. Step in as brand manager with, "Okay, let's park that concern and we can deal with it in the plan."

Your future brand is now taking shape. Your brand manager role is to keep it positive, possible and achievable so, once the flow is exhausted, it is time to refine.

As brand manager, ask questions like, "This objective of being a 'much-loved billionaire', can you be more specific? Do you think this achievable in 24 months?"

I often see generalities in this stage of the process, but that's normal. Identify the generalities and have fun exploring them as brand manager. So, if you've written "leader", explain further – leader of what, leader of whom? If you're the leader, who is following you?

Keep going until your future brand has some clarity, is positive and possible.

Then we can move to the next exercise.

Exercise 3. Overcoming your limiting beliefs and creating your development plan

Let the brand manager go home for the rest of the day, her work is done.

Now as **you**, with all of your concerns and limiting beliefs, look at the whiteboard/large piece of paper and you should see:

- On the left is your current state or brand, warts and all.
- On the right is the aspirational you, your future brand.

By now you will have built up a cast-iron case for why the aspirational you can't be achieved. (You're not good enough, you don't have the right connections, and so on.) Relax, this happens to most people I coach. It's temporary, trust me.

If you look at the bottom of the whiteboard/paper there should be some space left.

In this empty space at the bottom, draw a straight line, starting to the left of the current brand column and extending across to the right of your future brand. Now, imagine that this line is two years long.

It's two years long for a reason.

Starting at the left-hand end of the line, write down the things that you have to overcome in order to move your current brand toward your future brand. By this I mean the blockers preventing you moving forward. Things like training, either in personal skills like project management, coaching and leadership or technical skills like software applications and upcoming engineering systems. Think about what you would have to prove you have a capability in, like managing people or budget responsibility. It won't be hard to identify what's needed because your internal voice will be telling you that you can't do it.

Once you've identified the things that will underpin your move to the future brand, step back and look at the list.

Something should be quite apparent; you can't possibly do all this whilst delivering your current job. You don't have the time. (If your list is quite small and seems easy enough to achieve, then you haven't been honest enough – otherwise you would have done it by now.) There may be elements in this list that are not possible to obtain within your own organisation. Don't worry, that's common.

Take each item that needs to be achieved in turn and break it down. Are there elements that would be achievable if your current role was changed slightly? Say, for instance, by taking on more responsibility? Asking your manager for a discrete action that they could offload to you? Asking them to delegate more?

If the element is training, what training resources are at your disposal? Has your manager got a training budget? Does the organisation have a training programme? Find out and assess how you could access it – in my experience, most good managers would fully encourage this behaviour.

Are there elements of this list that are to do with experience? If so, don't panic. First, seek a mentor in the area that this particular element is focussed. Plus, seek to be a mentor to others.

If it's something hard to access in your current role, like team leadership or people management, then think outside the box. Does your organisation have a graduate training programme? If so, can you get involved as a mentor yourself? What temporary cover opportunities exist in the management team?

Keep iterating through the list of actions until you have a fleshed-out plan. This plan needs to have dates by which the elements will be completed, and this timeline has to be completed before the 24 months is up.

Now you have a plan that will account for the available time that you can invest over and above your current role, can be achieved by you (and not a superhuman) and has a clear purpose.

It's worth looping around this "clear purpose" issue because it is likely that one of the voices whispering to you will have continuously pointed out that you've done this stuff before and didn't stick to it.

Here's my response to that voice. Have you ever been through a process like this exact exercise before? Have you ever had a development plan in the past that had a clear purpose that was yours and not your bosses? Probably not.

This is *your* personal development plan and its purpose is to get you to where you want to be in a sensible timescale. Achieving it is now a matter of whether you believe in it.

Believe in your future brand

If you don't believe that the future brand that you have created is possible and authentic then we have a problem. If you don't believe that the future brand that you have created is authentic to you, then we have a problem. If you don't believe that the future brand that you have created is possible to achieve, then we have a problem.

If you're hung up on one of these issues, or you are just worried that if your peers find out what your aspirations are, they will disown you, then go back around the loop. Refine your future brand with the "authenticity" filter on and make changes. If you're struggling to accept that achieving your aspirational goal is even possible, then go back around the loop. Refine your development plan with the "possible in the available time" filter on and make adjustments.

Your plan to achieve the goal must be practical and realistic. If you're just hoping to achieve it, then go back around the loop, because you must want, even need, to achieve it. Otherwise you will fail at the first hurdle. If your plan requires you to spend the next three ~~months'~~ months of Saturday mornings reading and studying project accounting methods and techniques, then when your partner tells you to take the kids swimming one Saturday, you can't throw the book in the bin and say, "well, I tried!" and blame your failure on your other half. No one else is responsible for getting this done. Neither can anyone stop you.

Why is belief so critical? Because if you don't truly believe that it is possible to reach your goal, then you can't expect anyone else to believe in you.

Your future brand should be positive, visionary and, above all, achievable in a two-year window. It must also be *relevant* to the market. As brand manager, part of your job is to check this out every week. A couple of examples may help to understand how to do this.

One of my stellar performers had a plan to move her brand from principal consultant to architect in UK consulting services (a slightly different role). After a coaching session, she went out into her Hub network (see Chapter 4) with the intention of confirming the logic, or relevance, of her architect aspiration. Upon completing this exercise, she changed her future brand plan to cloud architect in a different part of the business. The Hubs she met gave clear and unanimous feedback that the future was cloud shaped. She was right, and successfully moved to this role in less than a year.

Another, less sublime, example was a coachee who was seen as a deep, deep expert in a complicated and widely deployed office productivity suite of products. His future brand was to become the "go to" consultant for the next big release of the product suite. As his coach, I felt that this was not a particularly exciting vision, but hey! I got him to agree to test the relevance of this future brand (as the brand manager) with some of his Hubs. The one Hub he spoke to agreed whole-heartedly with his plan and saw his future brand as awesome. They both left the company within 18 months when the particular product was canned. They were both arguing that the decision was wrong as they trudged toward the exit gate.

Trust me, testing the relevance of a future brand with your Hubs as often as once a week can pay huge dividends. But remember, this is about getting your Hubs' honest input and judgement on the relevance of your brand aspiration. Carefully choosing a Hub that will confirm your own bias won't cut it.

So, your brand manager can step away, but you must be able to call on them to test the relevance of your future brand as and when they're needed – ideally once a week.

Having done these exercises, what you've created is your FUTURE BRAND. This is your new personal development plan. It is relevant, achievable and it has a tangible vision. Record it for future reference but don't stash it away. Keep it to hand. You want to live it, not laminate it!

Your final test is this: when you read and talk about your future brand, does it excite you? Have you got an emotional connection to it? Does it resonate with you in your gut? It should, it will.

How *not* to make the most of your brand

There was a comic and sad character in a 1982 TV series *Boys from the Blackstuff*. It was about a group of fellows who laid road surfaces in tar (hence, the black stuff); they were out of work and finding it tough to survive but kept scrapping away. The character in question was Jimmy "Yosser" Hughes, played by the brilliant Bernard Hill. His catchphrase, borne out of desperation, was "Givvus a job, givvus a job!" and if anyone asked if he had a particular skill or relevant experience, he'd invariably say "Givvus a job, I could do that, I could do that!" – no matter the job. He was desperate and a little bit deranged but had an impressive moustache.

My point is, Yosser's desperation was his brand. Not a brand to elicit confidence.

<u>When brands become damaged</u>

It's surprising, but not unusual, for our emotions to get in the way of putting our brand across properly. We don't need to be desperate like Yosser, we only need to be frustrated, angry or anxious for our inner three-year-old to make an appearance.

In these situations, we tend to fixate on what's front and centre to us. Loss of amenity, loss of opportunity, loss of security can become the only thing important to us, which is completely understandable. However, in the wrong situation, it can be damaging to our brand.

Take the open microphone scenario at company meetings. "The leadership team is open for questions," says the MC. What they should have said is, "The land mine is now available for you to leap on!"

Been to one of these meetings? Remember the individual crusader who believes he is speaking for everyone in the room? Remember the feeling in the pit of your stomach?

Are you one of the ones who cringe when you recognise the person standing to ask a question? Or are you one of those that thinks, "He may well destroy his career but it might benefit me in some way ... or it could just be funny!"

And then comes the question...

"Will the closure of two branch offices and the redundancy of 50 of our colleagues delay the decision to improve the company car scheme?" Genius! (And a real, albeit paraphrased, question I heard once.)

If you're in one of these uncomfortable loss-related places, be infinitely more diligent about your brand. Avoid open microphones (that's a general rule for everyone, by the way) and take time to plan and settle yourself before meeting a Hub (see Chapter 4). Remember, the impression you leave is the one that gets communicated around the network.

I have worked with people, both men and women, who have a damaged brand in some sense. Either they have hung on to a dwindling wave for too long and been side-lined, or they got themselves into a bad situation on a project or initiative and became tainted by it. Another great brand killer is chasing something shiny and later having to return to the fold when it failed on you.

Fixing a broken brand is possible but it takes time, a long time, and a concerted effort – this is reason enough to avoid damaging your brand in the first place.

<u>What Jeff did wrong, and how we fixed it</u>

A case in point was Jeff (name changed to protect the guilty). Jeff led a difficult project in the Defence sector for Microsoft. The project team was the best, the project was very visible and the final outcome was seen as successful. Can you sense the "but"? To make the deadline, Jeff needed the team to go on a "death march", pulling 16-hour shifts, working over the weekend and late into the evening, or even all night. This went on for two months. Jeff presented the project to management as well within control, on time and on budget (he felt he had to "prove" himself). However, after the project ended, the team were asked for feedback on Jeff (standard practice in Microsoft). The feedback was not good. Two developers were off sick through stress, not one member of the team gave positive feedback on Jeff's leadership style and the client indicated that the approach taken by Jeff was "worrying".

Jeff came to me some months later, when the brand damage was hitting him hard; developers didn't want to work for him, program managers were slow to trust him and management oversight was intense. Consequently, he believed his career plan was now busted, the roles he had gone after disappeared and he felt like he should fall on his sword and leave (none of which was true). His manager referred him to me (known as a "hospital pass").

It was very clear that Jeff's current problem was twofold; yes his brand was battered (not as much as he thought), but his self-critical nature was doing the rest of the damage for him. At Microsoft, we are all encouraged to be self-critical and to focus on self-improvement. This is not what Jeff was doing. Self-improvement had morphed very successfully into self-destruction.

I coached Jeff on his brand first. To move forward, he had to be his own brutal brand manager and be totally clinical in describing his current brand (without muddy boots trying to justify how it happened). This took the longest and was a very emotional journey. However, Jeff came good. He got back some of his brilliant sense of humour and was able to be brutally honest with himself – the brand manager role helped put some distance between the hurt Jeff and the truth (as the brand manager saw it).

Once we had cleared the air and agreed on his current brand, the fun job could start: defining his future brand. What became very apparent in this stage was the current brand HAD to be incorporated in the future. It had to address what had gone wrong.

This works, and if done properly, it works extremely well. (Think of how George Michael "owned" his arrest for lewd conduct by officially coming out and satirising the incident in a toilet-themed music video.)

Jeff's future brand incorporated the scars that he gained from his experiences and, if there's one thing I know about the consulting business, scars are the most valuable commodity going. Customers pay for your scars because you will want to avoid them in future.

Scars became the component of Jeff's future brand that made his aspirations believable. It was breath-taking and it worked better than I expected. Within three months of Jeff promoting his new brand, he moved roles to the Major Projects team in Redmond as a director. They wanted his future brand and believed the scars underpinned this.

How stellar career performers make the most of their brand

Observing a stellar performer manage their brand turned out to be easier than I expected. I believed that they would hide their brand aspirations and be surreptitious when practising the dark art of promoting their own brand. I was wrong.

The stellar performers I met almost always were happy to share their plans and aspirations – some were a bit vague, others were crystal clear. I'm now sure this was partly due to the fact that I used the secret Hub handshake (see Chapter 4). Whatever the reason, they viewed my interest as valuable.

I also observed more direct behaviours that revealed some of their thinking. On a number of occasions, I observed stellar performers in an unproductive or negative meeting make excuses and leave (the old "hold the mobile phone up to your ear, mime to the room that it's important, and shuffle out the door" trick). On still further occasions, I witnessed stellar performers "working the room" at town hall meetings or larger office events with senior managers present. Their strategy was not to take the direct route, no, that was left to the numpties in the room who felt that bothering executives was a valuable use of time. The stellar performers used the situation to identify the executive's Hubs, and this is where they invested, and promoted, their brand. Listening in (which isn't difficult – just be nosey), they always made a Hub approach but steered the interaction toward their perspective, looking for brand relevance. This is where your clarity and rehearsal of your future brand, from this exercises in this chapter, come in handy.

One other place the stellar performers came forward was when opportunities to present a subject to a large company gathering, like monthly group meetings and off-site meetings, came up. Stellar performers were always willing to take these tasks on; they invested time and energy into their presentations and always (and I do mean always) managed to weave their future aspirations into the narrative – be it leadership, people skills, a technology or just raised profile. This way, they were working all three of the WaveMaker strands into their activity: awareness of their needs, cultivating their brand and harnessing the organisation's secret network. There's more on that last strand coming up in the next chapter.

Notes

Chapter 4. Infiltrating the secret society in your organisation

There absolutely is a secret network at work in your organisation – this is how to use it.

We all know how to do "networking", right? Networking is something we do when we can make time and space for it, right? We go to networking events or we go to conferences to network, right? We do this in the hope of something wonderful happening. We invest time in networking in the hope of tapping into some mysterious force or secret society that might do us good. As a by-product, we meet some interesting people.

Okay, but if you really want to find the secret society that operates within your organisation, where do you think you should look? At these networking events and conferences … or right here, in your own organisation? Right here, of course. But where is it hidden, where can you find it? You'll find it hidden in what's always the best place to hide something: in plain sight!

The secret society is there, right in front of your eyes. In fact, there are thousands of them. In fact, you're already part of a large number of them. I know, shocking isn't it?

If you aren't convinced, let's take a step back and look at this another way.

Introducing your extended network

The last big decision you made was probably buying a car. The way we buy a new car is universal – we research, we compare online, we visit dealerships and bother sales staff while telling them, "We're in the early stages, we're just looking, we're only considering, etc." We know not to trust sales people completely because they all want to "sell" to us. Being sold to is something we've learned through experience not to trust. So, once we've narrowed the field down, we all exhibit the same behaviour in one way or another – we seek the opinions of people we trust, people who we directly or indirectly know, who we believe to be unbiased, and who have direct experience of that make of car. Then we pump them for information.

Let's say we've decided to buy a new Range Rover. It's a reassuringly expensive car. It fits the family requirements that we have and looks the part. We also know that one of our neighbours had one a little while ago. We contrive to bump into them. We ask their opinion. They know someone who has the latest model, they're visiting next week, come over and have a chat, "they won't mind". You know that a work colleague has one, so you invite them for coffee and just so happen to raise the subject.

The interesting thing about this process is not that we all tend to do it, it's what happens next...

If you get a completely positive response from everyone, your buying decision is reinforced. You feel positive about your decision and are likely to proceed. However, if just one of these trusted resources gives a negative response, you aren't quite so positive. If two people give negative responses, it can put you off completely – even if there are an equal number of good responses.

Why is that? Well, it's partly because a new component has been added to your decision/risk equation. It's also because, if you go ahead and buy, and have the same issues, you look stupid.

So, coming back to our secret societies, who were the people that you went to for information? Why did you seek them out? What made their opinion so powerful?

The people you went to are part of your extended network.

The reason you made them part of your extended network was *ease of connection* (you knew them or they knew someone who knew you). They were *relevant* to the subject in hand. Plus they were available (*ease of access*).

They are, as defined by Dr Albert-Laszlo Barabasi in his brilliant book *Linked*, Hubs In your extended network. Barabasi (a physicist who has published a number of books on networking) defines the topology of all human networks as a star-like structure made up of Hubs joined together by spokes. This structure is universal to all human networks.

Understanding the rules that govern all Hubs

Hubs form the structure of these "secret societies" (networks). What's more, according to Dr Barabasi, all Hubs are governed by the three rules: ease of connection, relevance and ease of access (time).

We are all Hubs in some way. We all exhibit the above traits as we all have our own personal networks. However, Hubs are exceptionally good at it (high levels of connectedness, for example) and invest time in nurturing and maintaining their networks. Plus, and this gives them a much bigger advantage over many of us, they constantly seek out other Hubs.

Hub behaviour is also incredibly rewarding; the better you are at it, the more rewarding it gets. Rewarding both in terms of information and also financially.

Think about where you fit in the hierarchy of your organisation. Now, in your mind's eye, look up. All of those you are looking up at, right to the top of the board of directors, are better Hubs than you. They're better either through their skill, or through more experience.

How do they do it? They know the *secret handshake*.

A secret what?

The secret handshake isn't just a fetish thing for secret society members. It has a purpose. And that purpose is to identify, quickly and easily, other members of the secret society. In a Hub network, the secret handshake performs a very valuable purpose of identifying other Hubs. But before we get into that, we need to explore Hub networks and behaviours in a little more detail.

As I said, Hubs seek out other Hubs constantly. This is because what is flowing in the Hub network is *information*. Information is the lifeblood of any Hub, and the mechanism for this information flow is fascinating. The Hub behaviour that drives this information transfer is something called *reciprocity*. Reciprocity is something we all know about and encounter daily; if someone you know gives you something that you value (irrespective of whether they valued it at all), you are honour-bound to return the favour asap. If you don't, you feel guilty or you are a sociopath.

Reciprocity is what drives the Hub network. Hubs seek out other Hubs to access more information and they use reciprocity as the motivation.

If someone should tap into the Hub network and *not reciprocate* then they are a *leech*. Leeches are all around us, and they would happily suck a Hub dry without repaying the gift. Leeches not only steal information for free, they also steal time from the Hub that could otherwise be invested in genuine Hubs.

Stealing time from a Hub is the worst thing you can do because it impinges on one of their key behaviours: *connectedness*. If a leech is burning up the Hub's time, then that Hub can't connect with other valuable Hubs. And if they aren't reciprocating with other Hubs, then the value of their information is diminished (as they aren't connecting with the *relevant* information). Thus, their Hub value is diminished. The poor Hub dies on the network – withers on the vine, if you like – because their relevance fails, their connectedness fails and they were too easy to access by leeches who burned up all their time.

Time is one of the most critical aspects governing the Hub; they need time to be easy to access, they need to have been a Hub for long enough for other Hubs to find them, and they need time to invest in being a Hub. The more successful they are, the less time they have.

That's why there's a secret handshake. *The* secret handshake.

The beauty of a secret handshake (as any Mason will tell you) is that it makes it very quick and simple to identify another Hub (or Mason). By default, it's just as easy to identify a leech (or muggle – probably a term used by Masons). Note: not all Hubs are Masons, but all Masons are Hubs.

The secret handshake used by all Hubs is lightning fast and 95% accurate. The crazy thing is, you, dear reader, use it all the time without realising. You do, you know, and I'll prove it to you.

<u>Gaining access to the club</u>

Remember I talked about the way many of us go about buying a car? Remember our attitude to being sold to? Most of us rightly get suspicious of the seller's agenda.

Some of you may have been on training courses on how to sell and the value of your "elevator pitch". Your elevator pitch is the theory that, should you catch an unprotected client executive on her own in the lift, you can get across the key points of your product or service before she manages to escape, just after you tuck your business card behind her ear.

What a Hub is looking and listening for, in the first encounter with anyone unknown to them, is leech behaviour. Leeches invariably try to sell themselves. They try to be interesting!

A Hub, on the other hand, when encountering a potential Hub will be *interested*.

It's as simple as that. This is why the secret handshake works so quickly and efficiently. The even better news is, we all already know how to use it.

Don't believe me? Next time you make a plan to meet with friends for a meal or a drink, try doing the following. Arrive nearly last, then, when you approach your group of friends, immediately start telling them about how clever you are, how successful you are in your job and how wonderful your life is. Don't ask how they are, just broadcast your immense wonderfulness.

How long will it be before your friends tell you to shut up? Not long is my experience. If you ignore them and keep bragging, it won't be long before they shun you, refuse to speak to you and hang up on all your calls … in my experience.

My real point here is, that you would never behave like that with your friends. You would ask them how they are, how their family is, how the new job is shaping up, and so on. You would be interested. Anything else would be too uncomfortable and embarrassing.

So why are we trained to use an elevator pitch and sell ourselves? I don't know.

One argument is that we are meeting busy people who don't have time for chit-chat. The problem with that is that it assumes we are not busy and we do have time for idle chit-chat. Which we don't – our time is valuable too.

Ask any good, experienced sales person how they sell successfully and they'll basically say, "shut up and listen. You've got two ears and one mouth, use them in that order!"

So how can we use this piece of advice to signal our Hub potential to other Hubs? I'll show you a simple trick. In your organisation, as in all of the ones I've worked in, there is a universal capability that everyone has to demonstrate, on numerous occasions, to get hired. Can you guess what it is? It's never mentioned, never listed in the capabilities for the role or job description, and never objectively measured, but if we don't demonstrate it, we won't get the job. What is it?

It's *the ability to talk about ourselves*. Some find it difficult in interviews and have to learn to overcome their fears, while others find it all too easy and need to learn to moderate it, especially when nervous. Either way, you don't get hired if you can't talk about yourself.

You won't be surprised to know that most of the people in your organisation are good at, and comfortable with, talking about themselves. So, when you arrange to meet a Hub, simply talk to *them* about *them*. Be *interested* in them. If they are a senior manager, they will love telling you about their business and how it is faring, so ask them about it.

All human beings (except Trappists) love to talk about themselves. (In my case it's my grandchildren – ask me about them and you'll be hard pressed to shut me up.) By asking open questions about them, you are immediately showing Hub behaviour.

And that's it. You're in. You've gained access to the secret society.

Functioning Hub networks

As these Hub relationships develop and reciprocity is demonstrated, another aspect of the Hub network develops: *trust*. You have to be trusted by your Hubs for them to trust you in their own Hub network. Trust is a very powerful component, which explains the secret handshake.

Here's an example. You might even have had a similar experience to this. Say you have this brilliant, stunning and world-changing idea of how to streamline the back-end order processing, email confirmation system. You approach the head of Global Sales (and why not?) to explain it and get her buy-in. She listens briefly and then says, "Well, that's a really interesting idea, thank you for bringing it to me. I am currently focussed on increasing our sales profitability, but I know that Norman Numpty is working on the same area. I think your idea complements his. Why don't you get together with him, put a proposal together and come back to me in a couple of months?"

You go away with a spring in your step, intent on finding this ally with the full backing of the head of Global Sales. Happy days!

What a nice person she is, so approachable, so helpful.

But. Was she?

In the above scenario who is the Hub? The head of Global Sales (goes without saying).

Who is the leech? Norman Numpty (the clue is in the name).

Were you a leech or a Hub?

Unfortunately, you were a leech. The head of Global Sales simply disconnected with you, connected you to another leech and moved on. Elegant, eh?

Has this ever happened to you? It's happened to me in the past, for sure.

You obviously triggered the secret handshake alarm by trying to interest her in something she wasn't interested in. Had you been a Hub, you would have asked what was top of her agenda, found out it was sales profitability, grassed up a couple of sales people who are fiddling expenses and been her friend...

Anyway, you get the point.

The above scenario tells us something else about good Hubs. By disconnecting with you in the way she did, you still feel good, know she is approachable, was easy to get access to and is clearly highly connected in the business. By her not wasting time on a currently irrelevant issue, she has time to focus on what is relevant, thus maintaining her Hub credentials.

The secret handshake is therefore "edge protection" security for the Hub's network. It's their firewall. This security aspect can also create an interesting behaviour, but more of that later.

That's why there's a secret handshake, and that's how it works.

We all do this, because we are all Hubs in our own sub-networks, and we all use the same secret handshake:

Try to be interesting = leech.

Being interested = Hub.

Interesting stuff, eh? (Pun intended.)

A simple exercise to develop your Hub credentials

Before we move on, and we will move on, I would like you to do a simple exercise for me.

Pick someone in your organisation who is fairly senior, in some part of the business that has little to do with you. It would be best not to pick the CEO/MD/head of the NHS etc., but someone who is in a part of the organisation that you know little about. Go fairly senior, but not too senior (the simple reason being, it will take longer for the most senior people to find time to meet you).

Ask them for a 30-minute meeting, and tell them it is for you to get a better understanding of how the organisation works. Okay? Scared? Don't be, trust me.

When you meet, either in a coffee area, meeting room or some other meeting space, introduce yourself. Then ask them if they could spend a couple of minutes describing their domain, the kind of problems they face and how their part of the organisation is doing so far this year. Any kind of open question that cannot be answered with a "yes" or "no" (or "GO TO HELL!!") will do. "How are you today?" is an open question that I've used a lot. Then...

SHUT UP!

Sit quietly and give them time to think. Watch what happens. They will begin to answer your questions (they may ask for clarity – if so, help them). They will begin to talk about themselves.

This is NOT the point of the exercise. What happens next is.

After they have spent a little time answering your questions they are forced, through the rigour of etiquette, to stop and ask you about yourself. This is the Hub dance. All good Hubs behave this way, they can't help it.

Respond to their questions and ask any supplemental questions that may arise. And that's it. Exercise over. Phew!

Not quite. After the discussion, think about how much you learned and what additional things were discussed after your initial open question. Notice, too, how the chat unfolded. Did the conversation stay rigidly on the organisational issues initially posed? Probably not. Hopefully, what you experience and talk about is what's *relevant* to each of you. This relevant topic gets brought out and drilled down into. The likely outcome of this will appear to be totally random, based on what was going through the mind of your conversation partner at that moment.

The real truth is, it's not as random as you might think. There is an underlying purpose to all of this, and it's not all down to dumb luck. The conversation is being driven by what's relevant to those taking part. This relevance works both ways. Both parties are continually "filtering" what's coming their way, looking for relevance, and they do this in real time as the conversation is unfolding. Think of it like this: in the depths of your brain is a little fiddler crab (this isn't a horror story, I promise). This little fiddler crab is checking everything that it hears and sees for "interesting" stuff. It is doing this filtering all the time you are conscious. The outcome of the crab's endeavours is posted into innumerable slots in your short-term and long-term memory, for immediate or longer-term use. What happens to this information is explained later in the chapter.

How *not* to infiltrate the secret society in your organisation

Being armed and dangerous with the secret handshake and the unerring intention of using it isn't sufficient to get you safely in the door of the secret network HQ. Remember I talked about the role of time? To properly be accepted as a Hub, you need to behave that way all the time, not just for the initial five minutes of the meeting.

Here's a case in point. I observed one of my coachees in a coffee area Hub meeting with a member of the leadership team (I was sitting close by, absorbed in my laptop and sipping a coffee). After the initial five minutes, which seemed to go well, I could see my coachee leaning forward into the space left by the Hub who was leaning back, out of the way. I also observed that the Hub started looking surreptitiously at their watch. The meeting didn't last long. I later quizzed my coachee on what happened. "It was really good," he said. "I asked how the new job was working out and then he asked me if I had heard about the proposed changes to the business (announced that morning). I said I hadn't and that any change at this time was a bad idea and talked him through how well things were working in my accounts." I asked what happened next. "He had to leave." Clearly more coaching was needed.

Too often I have observed interactions like this. The urge to get your point across can be compelling, if futile. Hubs don't tend to give their opinion unless asked.

Remember to be flexible with your "being interested" opening question. A colleague who was a WaveMaker-trained coach once told me about a funny encounter that one of his coachees had relayed. The coachee had set a meeting with a Hub from another part of the business (as part of his attempts to learn the handshake). As the story goes, the Hub was waiting in the agreed coffee area when our hero turned up for the meeting. In fact, the Hub had been there for the whole morning because they had a leg in plaster (skiing accident). Our hero was planning the "how are you?" opening gambit, but, on seeing the broken leg, thought better of it. Seeing that the Hub had been in situ for some time and was looking quite uncomfortable, he panicked and blurted out, "Why are you here?" As our hero had arranged the whole meeting, the Hub was duly nonplussed.

How stellar career performers infiltrate the secret society in their organisations

To better understand how this Hub networking idea works, let's look at things from the Hub perspective. After all, the best Hubs are all stellar performers.

Remember, reciprocity is the mechanism that drives traffic between Hubs, but there's another important factor we need to consider: trust. Trust is a very important thing to maintain for a Hub; it's what keeps the freshest, most relevant information flowing. There are different classes of trust in a Hub's network, as well; some Hubs are highly trusted, some not so much. Maintaining the trust of other Hubs is also critical. This is where the secret handshake comes in again.

All Hubs are responsible for the security of the network. They will not let a leech loose on their Hub friends and will only refer an unknown or very new connection with caution. The reason is fairly self-evident as any contact or referral to another Hub implies judgement – the judgement of the initiating Hub.

Hub networks are very unforgiving in this aspect.

Also, Hubs can't waste too much time chatting with leeches as it's unproductive and drains the time they have to be available to other Hubs. And if they're inaccessible to other Hubs, their relevance to those other Hubs becomes diminished. This is why, when a new potential Hub approaches an established Hub, they are assessed with the secret handshake, and handled cautiously until they are a known quantity and more trusted.

<u>Getting a foot in the door</u>

Let's consider an imaginary Hub network: John, Pardeep and Sven.

I have made an appointment with John, to open up a link to him. I have read this book cover to cover many times, and have coloured in many of the important parts, so I feel ready to join the Hub dance. I meet with John, and reach out with an open question about him (the secret handshake). John doesn't know me at all, but responds positively to my clever opener, "Ummm, ahhh, how are you today, John? Ummm, errr, can you tell me a bit about your part of the business, please? I'm new and keen to understand." John then answers my question and is bound by the rules of etiquette to ask me an open question.

And we're off and running.

There is something very interesting happening in the background of this conversation; John is wondering what my agenda is. I, on the other hand, have no agenda other than to connect and interact. However, we are *both* processing what's being said, searching for something jointly relevant (we can't help it).

When the meeting is over and we have parted, we both share relevant pieces of information with our own Hubs. But more on that later. For now, let's assess what actually happened in the meeting between myself and John...

John has agreed to meet me for two main reasons. Number one being, it's the right thing to do (etiquette). Number two, he likes to meet diverse people from across the business because he learns things from them. There is a third reason at play, as well – I might turn out to be a valuable Hub.

Once I get through the secret handshake stage, John can relax his guard (partially because, thanks to this book, I have learned how to hack the Hub network, or, more likely, because I accidentally forgot to deliver my winning elevator pitch).

However, I seem to John to be showing interest in his answers. So when he's done talking, he asks me about myself, my role and maybe even my aspirations. And we're off on the dance.

The interaction now starts to change. John goes into "filter" mode (remember the fiddler crab?) and starts to pick bits out of my answers, storing them away for future use. What triggers his interest in some of my responses? *Relevance*.

Relevance is key

Let's look at relevance for a second, as I've used this term a lot, and we all assume we understand it. But, relevance is much more slippery than we think.

I used to think of relevance as being like the all-important company mission (that I have a laminated copy of, naturally) – as in, it's something concrete, static and easy to identify. But I now think of relevance as more like the aurora borealis – it's like a living thing (which, sadly for me means it can't be laminated). Relevance ebbs and flows through the organisation in shifting waves and powerful currents. It can't be seen, but its effects are immense ... and fleeting. What was relevant to someone when they got out of bed in the morning will probably have changed by the time they get to their workstation. We have texts, emails, messenger notes and phone calls all coming at us at what feels like the speed of light. We're all equipped with the means to access this information through our smart phones constantly, 24x7x365. We all know that to leave your phone un-glanced at for more than 10 minutes means WE DIE!! Even on holiday. Especially on holiday.

All of this stuff drives the *speed of relevance* in the 21st century and beyond.

John is keenly aware of this.

I look at it like this ... as I am talking, John is chopping up the information (sparse though it is) into packets. He is also putting a tentative label on each packet – for immediate or later delivery – or passing information into his long-term memory. Some of it he just discards (who needs to hear about my haemorrhoids, anyway!).

Incidentally, I am doing precisely the same thing.

Here's why. The information flowing between us is rich with information, much of it relevant. This relevance is both personal and business, short term and long term. Some of it will need to be handled immediately, some can be used later. This relevance is the feedstock of reciprocity. It has currency and value. From the perspective of the listening Hub, it also represents something else: it represents your brand. Your brand is how you are perceived by the Hub. It is what the Hub takes away from the meeting.

And you do exactly the same thing in your interactions. Take a moment to think about the last 30-minute conversation you had in your workplace. You were probably doing the exact same thing.

As the exchange continues, John identifies something I said that's really relevant to him. He wants to know more. As it's relevant to me (after all, I brought it up) we both happily drill into the subject. From the outside, an observer of our little tryst will notice a few things: John has leaned his head to one side (the international standard signal for "I'm listening, carry on"), we have moved our bodies slightly so that we're facing each other, and we're both slightly leaning in.

All good stuff.

Passing on relevant information

Now, the really critical behaviour of a Hub in this scenario happens just after we both part.

John picked up a couple of things that he thought were relevant. One thing was very relevant to his close colleague, Pardeep. In fact, it is something that she will probably need to know asap. Fortunately, as he passes the lifts, he sees Pardeep stepping out. He signals to her, she joins him and they have a quick conversation. She informs John that the snippet is very useful, but she recently passed the problem over to her colleague Sven. Sven is not someone that John knows well but she asks if it would be okay to pass the information to him, along with the name of the source. John agrees and they part.

On returning to his workstation, John finds a second to type an email to a colleague in the US to pass on another snippet that he picked up from me.

In six months' time, John will be in a meeting about resourcing a project and will recall that I mentioned my experiences and desire to manage a larger development project, and passes this info on to the hiring manager...

I am aware of none of this.

However, I have also just done something very similar, with all of my contacts. Hopefully you're familiar with this type of scenario, and you recognise that the more relevant the information is, the quicker the medium you choose to pass it through. (The most pressing is shared in person or on the phone, for example.) So, the hottest piece of information was passed on to my colleagues as soon as possible, because we all need to know that Diet Coke is being dropped from the coffee bar stock, in favour of Diet Pepsi! I know, it's shocking, and without any consultation!

I digress.

All of the interactions that John has with other Hubs, and which packets of information he passes along, through whatever medium he chooses, would appear to be completely *random*. Pardeep could have been out of the country or on vacation and he would have missed her. In turn, Sven would have missed out on the valuable information he needed. John's US colleague may miss John's email. Six months later, when the project resourcing meeting is held, John could be off sick with severe flu (a cold), and my name never gets mentioned in the meeting. You see? Apparently random.

However, I believe that there is more purpose and less randomness than you might think. The underlying activity of the Hub network is constant and unstoppable, the hunger for relevant information to feed the reciprocity mechanism is insatiable. The need to transfer this relevant information in a timely way is critical. If those key moments in time are missed, because colleagues were away or overlooked an email, John's need to make use of the information would have overcome those simple wrinkles in time. Not for any mysterious reason, but because the Hub structure is a resilient and self-correcting network. John and his Hub network would have found a way to get the information he gleaned from me to the destination Hubs reliably and in good time.

Unfortunately, it's also worth noting that I will never be able to find out what snippet of information was sent to whom. I can't go back and ask John what he did with any of it, it's not polite. I can't know what John found interesting or relevant from our meeting. Or can I? Cue super villain laugh … mwaaa ha ha.

Turns out there's another habit that Hubs have. Even though they protect their network from leeches, they have also developed an age-old method to bypass Hub security when it suits them.

Again, like the secret handshake, it's quick, simple and very effective. Hubs do it all the time. It's actually a good way to identify them.

Overcoming Hub edge protection security

Remember that Pardeep passed the snippet of information that John gave her over to Sven? Sven decides that he wants to follow this up and find out more from me. But, he has no relationship with me. How can he make direct contact with me without me thinking he's a leech?

Well, you'll be pleased to know that it's happening all the time to you already. In fact, the answer is probably sitting somewhere in your inbox right now.

Sven sends an email to me directly but, in the opening line, he must reference the point in the network that he knows I have a Hub relationship with, i.e. John. He will reference John, and possibly the route via Pardeep that the information took. You will no doubt receive some messages using this protocol to overcome your own Hub security. You will also follow this protocol when you are doing the same "hop" across the Hub network.

Anyway, this contact by Sven is very interesting to me. Not only does it satisfy my own anti-leech security bypass protocol, it also tells me which part of my conversation with John sparked this relevance-based chain of events. I can find out what John found interesting in this packet of information and also which route it took through the Hub network.

However, this email from Sven represents something far more valuable to me...

It's an opportunity!

It's an opportunity to create a reciprocity link with another Hub. It's an opportunity to extend the reach of my own Hub network. But, more importantly, it's an opportunity for me directly. This opportunity is now unique in the world of opportunities. This opportunity is specific to me. This opportunity was actually *created* by me. How it got back to me was not as random as I once thought – there was little luck involved.

Provided I have stuck to my future brand narrative, then this opportunity could well help to further my future brand roadmap.

And I created it. On purpose. It wasn't really random at all!

And it's relevant to the organisation, otherwise John wouldn't have passed it on and Sven wouldn't have contacted me.

This is a potential career wave that I made for myself.

That's why it's called WaveMaker.

Taking Hub behaviour to the next level: Becoming a Super-Hub

Hub behaviour is incredibly successful. The better you are at Hub behaviour, the further it can take you. Not all Super-Hubs are CEOs but all CEOs are Super-Hubs. The WaveMaker approach best explains why this is. Effectively, it's a self-propagating loop, as shown in Figure 3.

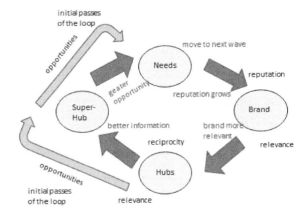

Figure 3. Hub behaviour in the WaveMaker loop

As you can see in Figure 3, the three main elements of the WaveMaker approach (needs, brand and Hubs) are represented. But a fourth element has now been added: the Super-Hub.

The first few times that one goes around the loop, the Super-Hub element is missed out. The Hub network promoting your brand creates opportunities that you assess against your core needs and either pursue or reject. However, as you get better at Hub behaviour, something happens. The more you iterate around the loop, the stronger your reputation in the organisation (or market) becomes; your brand is more relevant because you're honing it with better and better information because you're creating strong relationships with better Hubs. This makes you more valuable, which, in turn, creates a desire in other Hubs to interact more with you.

All this creates more opportunities but it also elevates the level of network interaction that your brand is exposed to – in other words, you get to interact with more senior Hubs. These Hubs are, by default, more accessible to you and your Hub reputation grows further. Now the information available to you to assist in honing your brand is newer, and critically much more relevant to the leadership of your organisation … and you have gone through a transition. Your Hub network grows outside of the organisation into industry, academia or government. You become a Super-Hub.

Interestingly, the one element in this loop process that hasn't change much is your core needs and values.

I have met with and served with Super-Hubs in all my roles. They are not necessarily CIO, CFO or CEO material. Maybe they choose not to go in that direction. However, they do exhibit such awesome connectedness that the CIO/CFO/CEO will know them (if they have any sense at all) and they will have influence at the executive level. As a result, these Super-Hubs have opportunities come their way that allow them to build fantastically interesting careers.

Notes

Chapter 5. The whole is greater than the sum of its parts

In Chapters 2, 3 and 4, we learned that the behaviour of stellar career performers points to a simple set of principles and activities that yield great results:

- *Fully understand your own needs and requirements from any role and don't compromise.* We do this through teasing out our "perfect wave" role, and understanding our five or six core needs or values LEDs.
- *Be completely responsible, clear and consistent with your own brand.* We do this by focussing on our brand and bringing out our "inner brand manager" to define how we want our brand to be perceived two years from now. To achieve this goal, we develop a plan to get us there via training, experience and mentoring.
- *There absolutely is a secret network in your organisation – use it.* We do this by engaging with Hubs, using the Hub secret handshake and developing our open question experience.

These are the three strategies I've seen employed by stellar career performers time and time again. But was there a bigger-picture, overall career strategy they used, as well?

This one took me a while to identify and understand. Unfortunately/fortunately, the answer came while I was trying my best to understand people who were failing. You see, many high achievers that fail in a role seem to do it for the best intentions.

This is where the saying, "The whole is greater than the sum of its parts" demonstrates the power of WaveMaker.

We've seen that the best surfers are the ones who can pick the best waves. The poor-performing surfers may have equivalent surfing skills but they either choose the wrong wave, join the good wave too late or, worse still, hang on to a failing wave for too long.

In contrast, stellar surfers, whilst riding a great wave, happily get off it and onto the next wave when the next great wave looks more promising.

This is true of the stellar career performers. They are able to spot their next career wave whilst riding the current wave to the full. Meanwhile, those with static careers find career waves to be scarce or non-existent, so they stay on the one they know, desperately trying to breathe new life into it.

In other words, I noticed that stellar career performers could see many more opportunities than those whose career was flat-lining. And they spotted the great opportunities time and time again.

How do the stellar performers achieve their repeated success?

Stellar performers practice all three components of WaveMaker simultaneously because they know that's what garners the best results. They know how to apply different parts of the trilogy tactically, but they employ all three elements strategically in the longer term.

Let me break it down into a simple timeline.

The stellar performers that I observed had a very clear idea about what they enjoyed and were good at in a role; they absolutely understood that it is their responsibility to take roles that support their needs fully. They invested time and effort into understanding their needs and assessing a role's suitability before they moved roles.

This process creates a positive reputation for the stellar performer. They are regarded as relevant to the organisation. They radiate success. Hiring managers actively encourage them to apply for their role.

Because they are riding a great wave, their energy and positivity is infectious. Other folk are attracted to them. Because of this, they can build great teams comprising the best players around them. This is self-breeding, self-sustaining behaviour of the best kind. Their reputation and relevance positively reinforces and boosts their brand.

While this is going on they are actively managing their brand, reviewing it, seeking feedback on it and polishing it where necessary. They are as sure as they can be that their future aspirations are underpinned by authentic results, not bullshit. In this brand management process, they are able to assess their brand's relevance to the organisation. They are also able to assess whether the organisation is capable of delivering on their brand needs. Because change is the only constant, they continually review and adjust their future brand to keep it fresh and relevant. They do this because they know that their future brand is the workhorse of their career growth.

Whilst they are doing this, stellar performers are feeding their Hub network. Reciprocity is the driver, so adding great information into the network is part of the deal but, for the stellar performer, getting great, relevant information back is the reason they do it. They invest time and effort in meeting new Hubs, promoting their brand further in the process. They rely on their reputation (as part of their brand) to underpin their brand's value. There is also seeming randomness at work here, moving their brand around the network, moving into unknown areas of the network and influencing yet unknown decisions.

All this is what the stellar performers are doing all the time. Now let's look at the effect this creates for them.

Stellar performer results

Because of this process, it is much easier for a stellar performer to stay relevant to the organisation. Due to the scope and freshness of the information coming to them, their brand management ensures that their future aspirations are in line with the organisation's. Their reputation grows stronger in the network but they also move their brand forward constantly to incorporate the needs of the organisation.

The forums that they present themselves in see the stellar performer as more relevant and more attuned (and thus more desirable). This attracts more Hubs, because strong Hubs want to increase the relevance of their own brand and knowledge. Hubs desire more reciprocity with the stellar performer, as their value is higher. Because it is so current and relevant, because it has kudos and value, other Hubs actively promote the stellar performer's brand around their own network.

This process of actively tuning their brand causes many more opportunities to come the stellar performer's way. More and more connections wishing to override the network's security protocols come their way. Because the stellar performers have a clear understanding of their needs (their perfect wave), they can pick and choose opportunities much earlier in the normal role development process. If they find a role that fits them, they are typically able to shape that role into their own. The reason? The opportunity that they chose to take was a wave created by their own activity, shaped by them.

That's why I call it WaveMaker.

Because you can actually create your own waves.

Notes

Chapter 6. How you can use WaveMaker for your own career growth

By now you should be fully up to speed on the underlying principles behind WaveMaker and the behaviour of stellar performers. You should understand the relationship between the three key elements of the formula, namely:

- Fully understand your own core needs and requirements from any role and don't compromise.

- Be completely responsible, clear and consistent with your own future brand, constantly honing it.

- Understand Hub networks, how they work and how to use them.

This final chapter is based on the practical advice that I give during my WaveMaker coaching sessions. It's designed to help you embed these ideas into your daily work life so that you can get the full WaveMaker effect.

Practical ways to understand your core needs

Following the exercise in Chapter 2, you should have your five or six core need LEDs labelled and recorded. You should understand the connection between these LEDs burning brightly and your own sense of well-being. Let's look at a few practical ways you can make the most of this knowledge.

If you recall, I talked about the effect that one or more LEDs flickering or going off completely can have on you, and how important it is to recognise this and take action. Easier said than done, though, eh?

We've all been in the position of knowing that "something isn't right" after a change has occurred at work. It might seem that a swift, post-work gin and tonic is the universal remedy to this feeling. But what should you do if the "something isn't right" feeling persists and the "just suck it up/have a gin" strategy isn't helping? Triple the dose of gin? Many have and will try this, and I'm not discounting it as a temporary fix, but let's look at some slightly more proactive approaches.

Calling on your Hubs

One approach is to exploit your Hub network. This is a situation where your own Hub network can help you, so make good use of it. There must be someone in your Hub network that you can safely approach on more personal issues, someone you trust. This Hub might not be within your own organisation, and that's fine. You'll know the best person to turn to.

You don't have to explain to them the ins and outs of your LEDs or the labels, but you can easily translate this into language you are comfortable with. Simply talk to them and ask their opinion. You'll be amazed at how insightful their observations and questions are. Why? Because what you are talking about is entirely relevant to them; they have careers, they have anxieties and they have experience. Their experience may not be completely relevant to your own but it will be relevant enough.

Get them to help you formulate an action plan. Remember, no action plan, no way forward. Include in the plan who to talk to on the issues, who NOT to talk to, when this needs to be done by and the outcome you are looking for. Ask your Hub to meet with you again in a week or so to review progress, and book that appointment then and there. This simple step can achieve two things for you. First, it has given you clarity because you have had to order your thoughts before describing the problem. Second, it has given you an action plan that will help settle your concerns. This approach will also give you more understanding and information about the situation that has caused your LEDs to blink.

In my experience, this simple approach can also alleviate stress. Stress is your enemy in this situation as it can spark brand-damaging behaviours like striking out at the perceived source of your concerns.

Reassessing your core needs

Another approach is to revisit your core needs process. Fish out the notes you made during the Chapter 2 exercise. Hopefully you will have a simple map for each LED, and what initial source feeling got you to that label. Now, spend some time calming yourself. If you feel emotional (and by this I mean pissed off or angry), try to let it pass for a second or two. In this next stage, emotions will get in your way.

Can you now think more clearly about which of your LEDs is either blinking out or extinguished completely? If a number of LEDs are a concern, try to pinpoint which LED started the cascade.

Here's an example from my experience as a coach. I was approached by a colleague and asked if I could spare them some time. I of course dropped everything and agreed to help (I'm a saint, plus, I was nosey and wanted to know what the issues were). They explained that they were unhappy with their recent performance review and had started to question their future in the business.

It turned out that the review delivered by their manager was focussed on one issue and one issue alone: their leadership style. It seemed that their manager was not interested in much other than this; their team's delivery performance, their recruiting success, their great team feedback … none of it seemed to matter.

When I asked to review which of their LEDs had gone out, they said all of them! So I asked if they could recall the LEDs that went out first in their meeting. They thought about it and got very emotional straight away. Hmmm … it was obvious that one of their core needs was very prominent and very damaged at that stage of the meeting. I asked them to try and calm down and breathe deeply and slowly. I asked about their recent vacation and their kids, anything to get their mind off the damage inflicted. Then, when they had calmed down, I asked, "What precisely did they say?"

And out it all came. Their manager had focussed on their leadership style, and had criticised them for being a "Servant-Leader", servicing and supporting their direct reports, instead of the "Business-Leader" that the new company direction required. And that was all my colleague heard.

What exactly a "Business-Leader" was, how they could become more "business-oriented", or what time frame they had to change in was never discussed because the damage was done in those first few sentences. The LEDs that went out immediately were now easy to identify as we reviewed their LED list. Valued was the first one mentioned and the first to blink out. Empowered was the next LED blasted into the dark, as their manager was saying they didn't support them and were likely to micro-manage them, and so on.

Focussing on Valued and Empowered, we developed a list of questions that my colleague wanted their manager to answer. These were:

- Valued – Is the leadership issue the only one that is causing problems? How serious is it as a problem? What, in your opinion, am I good at? What time frame am I looking at to address this issue? What resources and training will be made available to me?
- Empowered – Can I have an example of a great business-oriented leader in my role area? What reporting and feedback was needed to change this perception? Was this the perception of the business's management in general?

It was not that hard to develop a plan to address these questions. However, before we did this, I had an important question for my colleague.

As you can see from this real-life example, getting to the LEDs and the sequence of their demise is important. Understanding which LEDs blink out first can give you the questions that need to be answered, and give you your initial action plan. But, it can also tell you if the wave you are on is breaking underneath you, that your core needs will not be met. That's the time to employ WaveMaker to the full, find another wave, and move on with panache and dignity.

So, the important question I asked my colleague was this: "Do you really *want* to be a more business-oriented leader of people? After all, you aren't working in a sales environment and aren't especially aligned with one market sector, but you are aligned to a technology? Is the business's direction suited to you?"

This question really hit the mark. The emotion returned, and the frustration with it.

The answer to that question came a month later when my colleague moved roles in the business to a part of the company that valued the same things they valued, and viewed them as a huge asset. WaveMaker helped them achieve this fulfilling move.

Embracing the change

Yet another approach that can help bring clarity when change happens and your LEDs start to flicker is to embrace the experience with both arms. Treat the blinking LEDs as a wake-up call, smell the coffee, see the writing on the wall, stir your stumps, put on your walking boots and get out of Dodge.

There was an oft-used fable in the 80s and 90s about a frog in some water. Apparently frogs, being amphibians, don't have the ability to sense subtle temperature change. So, the fable went, if you dropped a frog into hot water it would croak loudly, look at you in a recriminating way and hop right out again. However, if you pop said unfortunate frog into cool water, it will croak, smile at you and swim around happily. It'll carry on doing this even if you heat up the water. It'll remain happy even when it boils to death.

This story was used by many people charged with the task of "change management" and was a particularly unsubtle way of letting you know that YOU were part of the problem!

But it turns out that the fable, when applied to people in organisations, is fairly accurate. There's a common tendency to deny that change is relevant to you. Over time, it becomes clear that another cliché is appropriate: "When the going gets tough the tough get going". The successful types tend not to hang around and wait for the end of the universe. The stellar performers heed their feelings of unease, and use their blinking LEDs as a trigger for change. They jump early.

You can do the same thing if you change the way you view your LEDs. Don't monitor them with trepidation and constantly hope that they don't start to blink. Monitor them like the huge asset that they are. Look out for the slightest flicker. View any fluctuation in your LEDs as the best type of earthquake warning system invented.

If any of your LEDs flicker, first understand which one is affected. Use this flickering LED to prompt a list of questions that need to be asked of your organisation (i.e. your manager and executives above them) to make sure that the organisation can still support your needs. Use these questions to create an action plan with short, hard timelines. If your core needs can still be met by the organisation, or if the cause of the flickering LED is not directed at you, then surf on. If you are left in any doubt, make your own waves!

Practical ways to be responsible, clear and consistent with your future brand

In Chapter 3, we covered the concept of developing your future brand. By now, you should have your first iteration of that future brand. You should believe that it's possible to achieve in the timescales discussed, and you should feel confident that your development plan can get you there.

To make this part of your daily behaviour and activity, there are a number of approaches that you can adopt to help move this from theory into practice. Again, each of these approaches are based on my experiences of coaching others.

Live it, don't laminate it

One approach is to explicitly take responsibility for your future brand by living it, not laminating it. By this I mean bring your future brand out into the open, share and test it with people. Having come from a technology background, I often encouraged the people I coached to pick an upcoming technology shift, or product or service release and become an unofficial spokesperson for it.

This led them to seek out the marketing people responsible for the upcoming releases (something I could help with through my own Hub network). Initial reluctance or concerns over being snubbed by those busy marketing people soon changed to elation when they saw that busy marketing types were delighted someone was willing to assist! This gave my techies the wherewithal and early release presentation content to be able to present the new stuff to their colleagues and clients. It also aligned them with those mysterious – but wonderfully budget-rich – marketing folk who were willing to put client deployment work opportunities their way (thereby increasing the consultant's utilisation and revenue). It was a win/win all around.

What my techies had done was bring their future brand focus forward and found a forum to display it.

If you think about it, this same outcome can be achieved with almost all of the elements of a future brand – technology-related or not. If you're explicit about what it is you are trying to portray, then vehicles for this will present themselves to you. Because you are looking for them, and, believe it or not, the vehicles are looking for you.

Making sure you don't get side-tracked

Another approach is to work on a clear and consistent delivery of your future brand. "Duh, that's obvious!" I hear you say. But it's not. I have seen first-hand how easy it is for someone to go "off-mission" with the way they present their future brand. It's not hard to get off track if something shiny comes along to excite you. It's not hard to get off track if the job you are delivering right now is burning all of your hours up. It's not hard to get off track if your immediate boss couldn't care less about what you are up to. But don't be disheartened. Go back to the work you recorded in the exercises in Chapter 3. Is your future brand still exciting to you? Has anything happened to stop you believing in it? Do you still want it?

The tendency for the immediate and critical needs of your organisation to take priority, the tendency for your manager's demands to be front and centre, the tendency for other interesting stuff to pop up all the time should be viewed by you as a tax on your future. Nothing more. Everyone has to pay taxes (unless you are … oh, I'll stop there before I get into trouble). But that is all they are … taxes. They are NOT a blocker. They are NOT a reason to give up your future. These particular taxes are the price of working where you have chosen to work, they are common to everyone working there, and if you aren't prepared to pay them, leave. However, bear in mind that, if you leave, you will not be moving into a tax-free environment. That only happens when you die (unless you're … no, I shouldn't).

This is the point where belief in your future brand comes to the fore. If you believe in your future brand and are excited by it, then you must find a way to make it a reality. If your first plan won't deliver things in time, then create another plan suitable for the environment and resources available. Keep reviewing your plan, not your vision!

Staying relevant to the organisation

Yet another approach is to constantly hone your future brand and its associated plan to ensure that it remains relevant to the organisation. This is a crucial element and is worth thinking hard about. If your future brand is no longer relevant to the organisation, you have one of two decisions to make: abandon your plan or abandon the organisation.

Hubs will be your greatest asset in honing your future brand and plan. Remember in Chapter 4 we covered the "currency" of Hub networks, and how relevance ebbs and flows through them and the organisation like the Northern Lights? When interacting with your trusted Hubs (more on this later in the chapter), you'll be given constant feedback on the relevance of your brand, provided you are clear and consistent when presenting it – by presenting it, I mean whenever you talk about yourself when Hubs give you the floor. Hubs deliver feedback all the time, they can't help it.

Listen very carefully to what your trusted Hubs are saying. There is no harm in asking a trusted Hub for their opinion on the relevance of your future brand to the organisation. No harm at all. But I recommend you get more than one opinion to avoid agenda bias in any one Hub. Hone and polish your brand based on this information. Ensure that your future brand is as shiny as possible. When coaching people, I would recommend that, after investing in Hubs, their next big career investment should be time spent honing their future brand. I would recommend the massive investment of 10 minutes a week, because that's all it takes. Surely you can spare 10 minutes a week?

Here's a great example of how just a few minutes a week can pay real dividends. One coachee's future brand was to become a recognised specialist in a particular systems management solution aimed at our corporate/global clients. In the future capability of this solution was a planned cloud-based service. However, the cloud service availability was slipping to dates that fell outside of his planned timescales and, as a result, he was getting despondent. In reviewing the situation with his Hubs, he discovered that the small business version of the cloud service was shipping first. He connected with the UK marketing team for this product, got roped in to their plan and became the lead consultant for this product release. The small business version of the service was almost identical to the large/global client solution in many aspects and put my consultant into the enviable position of being asked to advise the large client product team based on his experiences. This put him at his planned future brand outcome months earlier than he planned and catapulted him into the limelight before the service was actually launched! A great result from a slight change of plan.

Practical ways to understand and use Hub networks

I have said a couple of times that WaveMaker is all about applying all three components together to get the most effect. That is very true.

However, the coolest part of WaveMaker (for me, anyway) is Hub networking. Perhaps it's because I come from a technical background, and, more specifically, from a networking technology background (a long time ago, when dialup was still an option).

Hub networks are the engine behind WaveMaker. They supply almost limitless free energy (real, attainable, free energy, unlike zero-point energy) and run 24 hours a day, seven days a week and 365 days per year.

At an individual level, most of us understand Hub networking (okay, perhaps not Sheldon Cooper), because we are personally governed by the rules. However, exploiting Hub networks to your own advantage is alien to most of us because simple etiquette is burned into our subconscious from a very early age. If it wasn't so alien to us, Dale Carnegie's book *How to Win Friends and Influence People* would never have been such a smash. Because I'm a techie and I have to know how things work, I can't help peering under the bonnet and looking at these networks from a mechanical perspective. (I'll be putting this keyboard back together soon and it will work better.)

My words "exploiting to your own advantage" may seem calculating and manipulative. They are meant to be. If you stop thinking of Hub networks as individual people and think of them as a mechanism, then exploiting them for your own advantage becomes a lot like driving a car or riding a horse. Left to their own devices they will do what they do, but if you know how to manipulate them they will help you get where you want to go. Which is why horses don't drive cars.

Let's look at a few techniques for exploiting Hub networks to your advantage.

Deploying the secret handshake

One approach is to prove to yourself that the phenomenon of Hub networking actually works. The most powerful aspect of this is the secret handshake. If there is one aspect of Hub networking that the people I coached found hardest to absorb it was the simplicity of the secret handshake. To quote one of my consultants, who was Eastern European and notoriously blunt, "This is sounding like bullshits to me." However, even he agreed to try it out.

Remember, trying to be interesting is the trigger for disconnection (however elegant that disconnection may be). Being *interested* is the recognised Hub behaviour. The interaction that follows your opening "being interested" questions will give all the clues you need to your next "being interested" questions. Then, the rules of good manners means the Hub (if they are a Hub) will have to be interested in you. Simple. No bullshits.

I used to give my consultants simple tasks to test the secret handshake. You can try it too.

Pick a part of the organisation that you don't know very well (or at all). In the organisational map (there is always an organisational map – it's what intranets were made for) seek out either the person that runs it or one of their direct reports. Use email to make contact and ask for a short meeting (you will buy the coffee), explaining that you would like to better understand the business overall, and want to understand how their part of the business fits in. Nothing more, nothing less.

When you meet, use the secret handshake. Try something like, "Thank you for agreeing to meet with me. I'm fairly new to the company and would love to know more about the car park management section. Can you tell me what you do?" Remember, the unwritten capability of all employees is the ability and desire to talk about themselves, so sit back and listen intently. How long does it take for them to ask you about yourself? How soon in the meeting did you both identify something of mutual interest?

I have seen some fascinating results from this. One of my consultants met with a senior manager in the Search Engine group and ended up selling his Spanish house to them. My Eastern European friend had less luck; he met a fairly junior member of the Desktop Marketing team, who was quite new to the company, for a coffee. After the meeting, I asked him how it went. His response was, "As I thought, is bullshits. I ask her what she do, she doesn't shut up for 45 minutes, she never asked me question." What we learned from this was, she clearly wasn't a Hub, just an enthusiast.

<u>Finding the gold in your Hub network</u>

There are two strands to this approach. In the first instance, you want to carefully watch a Hub's behaviour when you meet them for the first time. Most of the interactions we have with one another when face to face are rich in nonverbal communication: body posture, hand actions and that old chestnut body language. If you spend your interaction time just looking for this, the meeting will soon end and "some kind of nutter" will be added to your brand. So, just look for, and get good at spotting, one thing: get good at spotting when you and your companion find something of mutual interest.

When a couple of people find something of mutual interest, things change. One or both parties lean toward each other, everyone else in the vicinity pales into the background, they become focussed. Learn to spot this and to mirror. This will help you get maximum value from the Hub network.

This thing of mutual interest may be nothing at all to do with work or the business. It may well be something personal, like my sailing enthusiast Hub from Chapter 1. Don't worry, go with it. You are not wasting your or their time. Once you both find something of mutual interest, conversation flows, ideas get exchanged and … a bond starts to build. A rudimentary trust is forming. That's why Hubs seek out other Hubs and how friendships blossom. Trust.

Now, as you get better at developing this, you can move to a more structured approach using a very simple technique. You can map out your Hub network.

Start by simply drawing circles with interconnecting lines and, in the circles, write the names of the individual Hubs. The circle in the middle of all of this should be you. This stage is important, but not the most important. You should be able to plot 10–15 folk that you consider meet the stellar performer Hub criteria laid out in Chapter 4: highly connected, easy and available to interact with, and relevant.

Now, regarding the lines you have drawn from your circle to their circles, think about the traffic (interaction) that flows between you and each Hub in your network. The greater the traffic, the thicker the line you should draw. Remember, this is not a map of your everyday work interaction; it should represent your own Hub network. This network will probably not map onto the organisational structure; instead, it will represent your own journey through the organisation and the trusted Hubs you are connected with.

Once you have drawn the thicker and thinner lines on this map, step back and look at it.

There is gold in this map. The gold lies not with the thick connections, but with the thin ones.

Remember how WaveMaker works. The thin connection lines show you the Hubs in your organisation who you haven't interacted much with recently. These people are trusted Hubs that you can connect with easily without worrying about network security, secret handshakes or nervous first questions. They are people who will be very receptive to you personally, but they are unlikely to know about your new future brand. They most likely just know of your reputation.

Fix this straight away! These Hubs are your greatest unused asset. Meet with them and update them on your brand. Just one of them could create your next wave.

Digging for more treasure … in your inbox

Another useful technique is to re-examine, and go mining for gold in, your email inbox.

Remember what we covered in Chapter 4 about how people overcome the "edge protection" security of Hub networks? This universal technique of mentioning your trusted Hub as the point of reference? Not only does this tell you that the person contacting you is a trustworthy connection, it tells you what snippet of information your Hub found relevant (because they passed it on to this connection), and hints at a potential direct opportunity for you. However, it also gives you another nugget of data – you can add the unknown person who contacted you as an extended Hub of the Hub you already knew. So, this is an unknown Hub who is connected to your Hub, and someone to add to your Hub map (I use dotted lines in these cases). This gives you a potential new Hub in a new part of the organisation. Whether you followed up the potential opportunity that they contacted you about or not, you now know their area of relevance and have a new Hub to potentially connect with again.

Now go back into your email inbox and look for something else. Are you a member of any social groups? I was a member of the sailing group (obviously). It's easy to identify who else is a member of these groups; the directory or mailing list will tell you. Are there any obvious Hubs in this list? If so, you've already got a mutual interest (you don't have to wait for your manager to "tip you the wink" like I did).

We haven't finished yet, as your inbox is a gold mine of potential Hubs, trust me. You can mine it for technology-relevant groups, management-relevant groups, socially-relevant groups and personal contacts, just for starters. Identify the folk that you have worked alongside, in projects with and been on training courses with. Rekindle your links to these folk when you have a quiet few minutes. Meet for a coffee or maybe send them a link to an article they'd enjoy. I once had a great role opportunity come my way via a friend who I exchanged topical jokes with!

Ultimately, you can view Hubs as an exhaustible resource that must be used sparingly, or you can view Hubs as a limitless resource with infinite possibilities. The WaveMaker knows the difference, and invests their time and energy accordingly.

Remember, in the modern corporation, it's not who you know, it's not even what you know, it's *who knows what you know*.

Notes

WaveMaker testimonials

I have found the WaveMaker process a fantastic way to coach people from all walks of life, and from those just establishing their careers to senior leaders. It has enabled my clients to get clarity on what makes them work at their best; to feel confident in being who they are and not trying to present themselves as something that is artificial; and to make genuine connections from that place. From a personal perspective, WaveMaker continually enables me to reflect and adjust the work I truly love doing. I just wish I'd know this years earlier.

My advice to make WaveMaker work for you is to read the book and work with a buddy, coach or mentor who can help you to step back and be truly objective. It can be too easy to pursue a career that is successful on the "outside" but doesn't feel the best fit on the inside. Life's too short to mess around.

Kate Burton

Author, Executive Coach, NLP Master and Trainer

I have been a manager in the IT industry for most of my career and have a real passion for helping others to realise their potential. In order to best do this, I have attended a lot of training over the years to build my people skills – including becoming an NLP Master Practitioner and a qualified coach. As well as leading my team, I am also regularly asked to be a mentor for others, with career development being a regular topic that mentees would like help with. I am a lifelong learner and love to discover new tools that will help people further develop their talents, find a sense of purpose and live life to the full. I enjoy this so much I even do it in my spare time, not just during working hours!

I was first introduced to WaveMaker by a colleague during a discussion about personal and career development techniques. I was immediately curious and keen to hear more and learn how to use this methodology myself as the description I heard sounded fully in line with my desire to help others realise their full potential.

In practice, I attended a WaveMaker training course and experienced for myself the power of WaveMaker. As we learnt the different tools that make up WaveMaker (for example, coaching methods and NLP techniques), we put them into practice by working with a colleague, taking it in turns to switch from coach to coachee. I was very lucky to have a great coach and I found myself very emotional at one point during the process. WaveMaker had clearly tapped into something deep for me – deeper than I felt comfortable exploring at the time, but highly valuable for me to reflect back on at a later point in time.

What did it deliver for me?

WaveMaker helped me get clarity on my own perfect wave, and having that knowledge has enabled me to change and influence my own career direction so that now I spend all my time in a learning and development role.

WaveMaker is probably the coaching tool that I most frequently find myself using as a manager and mentor. It has added value to everyone that I have used it with and has definitely made me more effective in both of those roles – helping others gain clarity on their own unique strengths and value, giving them a clear plan for the future and helping them to network effectively to find opportunities aligned with their strengths. Often they experience one or more "aha!" moments as they go through the process and gain the insight and skills to become WaveMakers themselves and create their own perfect waves.

My tip for making WaveMaker work for you? WaveMaker isn't a one-off process – take out your notes (book) and revisit it whenever you find yourself in need of a career boost. I regularly revisit my plan, check that my work environment is still providing the right conditions for me to thrive, and proactively reach out to add value to my network in order to stay on the right waves that will work for me.

Finally, to really embed WaveMaker, teach it to others – it takes your own learning to a whole new level.

Christine Clacey

European Development Manager, Microsoft Customer Services

About the author

Having learned a great deal about engineering as a draughtsman during a 4 year apprenticeship with Vosper Thornycroft (a builder of medium sized war ships) in Southampton, Robin moved into the water purification industry, designing treatment plant control systems. Later he moved into the petro-chemical industry again designing control systems. This is where Robin encountered computers, this discovery changed his career. Majoring in systems communication and shifting his focus to sales he was hired by Hewlett-Packard UK as a Technical Sales Rep. Mini computers and Micro computers where in the ascendency and the business boomed. Robin's knowledge of communications (which now included various types of LAN and WAN technologies) made his brand more and more valuable. A brief sojourn to Ungermann-Bass (chasing something very shiny) was the only interruption to a long career with HP. This career stage took Robin to country sales manager for healthcare computing. Upon leaving HP Robin ran a start-up business (Leo Systems) focussing on HP Unix Mini computers and Windows Server networks. Leo was bought and after a year of helping bed the Leo business into its new home, Robin left... to play golf for a month. The golfing was rudely interrupted when he was hired by Microsoft. Microsoft UK were seeking more experienced systems people at the time (1997) to add knowledge and grey hair to its multi-national client sales capability.

Robin again moved "upwards and to the right" within Microsoft UK every couple of years and held various positions in sales, global account management, sales management, project team management and finally as a professional development manager in the consulting services arm of Microsoft UK. In 2005, at the age of 49, Robin was diagnosed with prostate cancer which took a great deal of his time and focus to overcome. The cancer was in remission for 4 years when it returned, again taking time and focus to deal with. Robin's career took a back seat during this period, however he was still delivering the professional development role to the full. Cancer back in remission, Robin resumed his career, but in 2014 Robin's health problems returned with a vengeance as he was diagnosed with blood cancer. This effectively forced a change in lifestyle and focus.

Robin is a keen sailor, owning a beautiful example of the Westerly Merlin, but spends much of his time with his grandchildren, of which he now has six, three girls and three boys.

Robin has been a dietary vegan for 9 years changing his diet to help improve his health and is a keen cook.

Robin has been married to his darling Maggie for 44 years (he was a child bride).

To contact Robin with any questions or observations he can be reached on

robinfarmer@hotmail.com

Acknowledgements.

Kate Burton and the late Rob Biggin for their help and guidance in developing WaveMaker.

Christine Clacey for her undying support and backing.

Microsoft UK for giving me the opportunity and space to grow and develop WaveMaker and Anthony Saxby (my manager at the time) for encouraging me.

To my children, Matthew, Daniel and Kayleigh for being my guinea pigs.

To Claire Ruston at Wordegg... www.wordegg.co.uk ... for her patients and professional advice.

To my darling Maggie for everything else.

101

Notes.

Printed in Great
Britain
by Amazon